Shifra Stein's

Day Trips®
from Baltimore

Help Us Keep This Guide Up to Date

Every effort has been made by the authors and editors to make this guide as accurate and useful as possible. However, many things can change after a guide is published—establishments close, phone numbers change, hiking trails are rerouted, facilities come under new management, etc.

We would love to hear from you concerning your experiences with this guide and how you feel it could be made better and be kept up to date. While we may not be able to respond to all comments and suggestions, we'll take them to heart and we'll also make certain to share them with the authors. Please send your comments and suggestions to the following address:

The Globe Pequot Press
Reader Response/Editorial Department
P.O. Box 833
Old Saybrook, CT 06475
Or you may e-mail us at:
editorial@globe-pequot.com
Thanks for your input, and happy travels!

Shifra Stein's Day Trips® Series

GETAWAYS LESS THAN TWO HOURS AWAY

Shifra Stein's

Day Trips®

from Baltimore

Fourth Edition

Gwyn Walcoff
Bob Willis
Edited by Shifra Stein

OLD SAYBROOK, CONNECTICUT

Contents

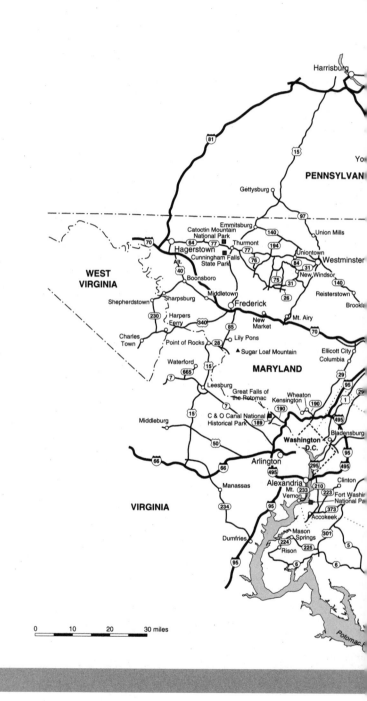

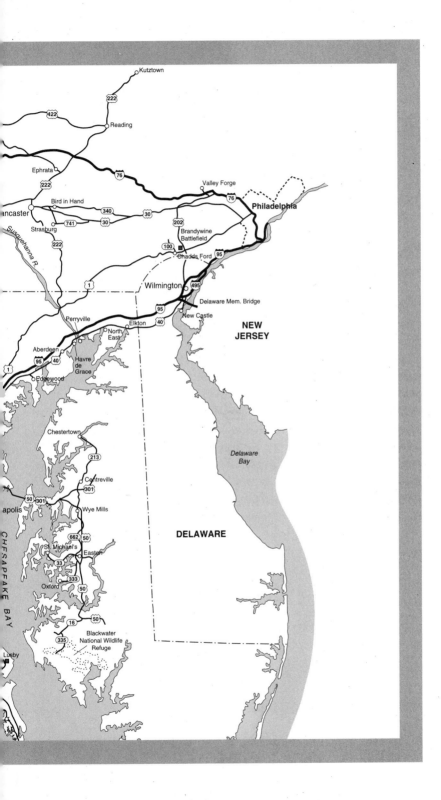

SOUTHWEST & WASHINGTON REGION

WEST

NORTHWEST

DIRECTORY

Preface

Welcome to Maryland, a beautiful area that has played a great role in America's history. Here cemeteries have headstones that tell the stories of Revolutionary War patriots, and chronicles of Maryland's past tell of visits by Spanish Jesuit missionaries as far back as 1570!

With this *Day Trips* guide in hand, you'll travel through three centuries of history in southern Maryland. Special places here pay tribute to the agricultural heritage that still predominates in the region. This guide will lead you to rich landscapes, past Maryland's horse country, and through the open fields and pristine farmlands that are part of the Pennsylvania Dutch area.

Along the way you can sample a variety of foods and Americana sold in wonderful shops and marketplaces that dot Maryland and the nearby states of Pennsylvania, Virginia, West Virginia, and Delaware—all colorfully outlined in this book.

From agriculture and architecture to history and high tech—it's all here, and it's all near.

HOW TO USE THIS BOOK

When using this guidebook, be sure to keep in mind the following:

Driving Time: Individual trips are designed as one-day, round-trip excursions with the farthest points within a two-hour drive from greater Baltimore. Sometimes the itinerary goes beyond that limit, as in the case of Charles Town. Such destinations are titled "Worth More Time."

Maps: While maps are included in this guide, we highly recommend taking along state maps for more detailed information.

Highway Designations: Federal highways designated as U.S. State routes are defined as follows: M for Maryland, D for Delaware,

P for Pennsylvania, WV for West Virginia, and V for Virginia. Interstate routes are designated as I.

Restaurants: Meal prices, not including beverage, tax, or tip, are designated as follows: $ (inexpensive—less than $8.00 per person); $$ (moderate—$8.00 to $15.00 per person); $$$ (expensive—more than $15.00 per person). The ☐ symbol indicates that credit cards are accepted. "No ☐" indicates that major credit cards are not accepted.

Hours: Because this guide must be prepared months in advance of printing, details such as hours and days of operation, which change frequently, could be obsolete by the time you read them. Therefore, we do not always include days and hours of operation; we do include telephone numbers so you can call for up-to-date information.

Combining Trips: These trips are arranged so they may easily be combined into an excursion of more than one day. In several cases you could take one trip out and another trip back, or you could combine two or more day trips in the same sector.

Festivals and Celebrations: Check the directory in the back of the book to find out what's going on in the area before you head out. Telephone numbers are included so you can call for specific information.

As always, your suggestions for future editions are welcome.

Shifra Stein

Acknowledgments

We gratefully acknowledge all help and assistance given to us by the chambers of commerce, state and regional tourism departments, and convention bureaus of the states of Maryland, Delaware, Pennsylvania, Virginia, and West Virginia, and of Washington, D.C.

Day Trips from Baltimore

North of Baltimore is the rich landscape of Maryland horse country. Mother nature is at work in the Boordy Vineyards and the graceful, green extravaganza of Ladew Topiary Gardens. As suburbs yield to rolling countryside, sprawling farms, meadows, and woodlands, you'll see some of the most picturesque countryside in the state.

Pennsylvania's south central area has the state's capital, Harrisburg, as well as the open fields and pristine farmland of Amish country. Here, horses and buggies still travel on the highways, recalling earlier times. This region's appeal isn't all history, though. Some of America's most enjoyable theme parks are located here. Fun for all ages awaits visitors seeking thrills and activities at Dutch Wonderland and Hershey Park. And (grab your pocketbook!) you'll be visiting the "Outlet Capital of the World." The York-Lancaster-Reading shopping triangle boasts a bounty of bargains.

Groaning boards laden with Pennsylvania Dutch cooking are a feast for the eyes and the appetite. Have your day trip dinner at one of the many smorgasbord-style restaurants featuring local traditional fare. Take home tasty breads and pies from the colorful Amish markets as you wend your way home from your trip to the north.

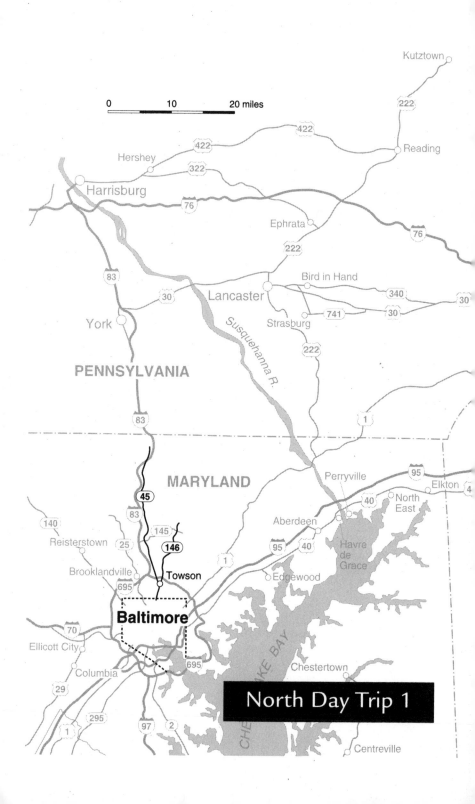

0   10   20 miles

Kutztown

222

422

422

Hershey

322

Reading

Harrisburg

76

Ephrata

76

83

222

Bird in Hand

340

30

York

30

Lancaster

741

30

Strasburg

222

PENNSYLVANIA

Susquehanna R.

1

83

MARYLAND

Perryville

95

Elkton

4

45

North
East

140

83

40

145

Aberdeen

146

Reisterstown

25

95

40

Havre
de
Grace

Brooklandville

1

Towson

695

Edgewood

Baltimore

70

Ellicott City

695

Chestertown

Columbia

29

CHESAPEAKE BAY

295

97

2

North Day Trip 1

1

Centreville

BALTIMORE COUNTY, MD

The northern corridor extends an invitation to sample scenes and sights of Baltimore County. Depart the city north on York Road (M–45) to Dulaney Valley Road (M–146) in Towson. We'll visit the natural beauty of a reservoir, the cultivated elegance of a topiary garden, and a vineyard and winery.

WHAT TO DO

Loch Raven Reservoir. Proceed north on M–146 from Towson for about 3¾ miles. Winding roads lead you through beautifully forested areas pervaded with the scent of pine. Breaks in the dense trees allow views of the 10-mile-long lake. The reservoir area, built in 1912, offers excellent picnic areas (no open fires), boating, fishing, and hiking activities. Saturday and Sunday visits are especially nice for bikers, skaters, and joggers because on part of the thoroughfare regular traffic is blocked. Terrain is varied, so physical exercise potential is good. Free. Over the past few years, an increasingly larger number of Canada geese have made this their year-round home. They have become quite tame and enjoy treats of bread and crackers. Call the Baltimore County Department of Recreation and Parks, Loch Raven Community Office, (410) 887–5309.

 Ladew Topiary Gardens. Located at 3535 Jarrettsville Pike (M–146), Monkton. After passing Jacksonville, watch for the topiary gardens. Twenty-two acres of artfully planned gardens await you. Cited by the Garden Club of America as America's "most outstanding topiary garden," it features fifteen seasonal blooming gardens. The world-famous topiary hedges feature a life-size topiary fox hunt with horse and rider. The hedges are clipped and patiently trained into the shapes of animals and other whimsical objects. The Manor House of the late Harvey Ladew, creator of the gardens, contains antiques, paintings, and objets d'art. The house and gardens are on the National Register of Historic Places. A craft and garden shop are on the premises. Often in the summer, there are Sunday concerts featuring everything from bluegrass to chamber music. From time to time, there are also polo matches on the grounds. For these events, you can bring your own picnic dinner (no fires) or purchase food and drink on the site. Fee. (410) 557-9466.

The Boordy Vineyards. Located at 12820 Long Green Pike, Hydes. Take Jarrettsville Pike (M–146) to Manor Road south and turn left. Continue on Manor to Long Green Pike east, and turn left to Hydes. Nestled in the hills of Baltimore County is the oldest vineyard in the state. The rustic barn surrounded by vineyards, stone patios, and pastures is a welcome departure from the fast urban pace. Here, grapes are picked, cleaned, crushed, and then aged in vintage oak casks.

Boordy produces a full line of dry table wines that excel at complementing food. They also offer a popular sweet variety of wine. The individual attention given to these wines includes hand-labeling each bottle. Production averages 5,000 cases a year. During the spring and summer season, there are often Sunday events taking place here, usually featuring a gourmet picnic luncheon followed by an extensive wine-tasting session. Knowledgeable guides direct visitors through the vineyards and winery. September visits are especially good, for this is the best time to see the harvesting and crushing. A picnic area is available. Notify Boordy in advance for group tours. No fee, but there is a tour charge for groups greater than ten. (410) 592-5015.

WHERE TO EAT

Peerce's Plantation. 12460 Dulaney Valley Road, 7 miles north of Towson. This scenic dining spot, located at the entrance to the watershed area of Loch Raven Reservoir, offers consistently fine food. The dining rooms have a view of the lake. $$$; ☐. (410) 252–3100.

The Manor Tavern. 15819 Old York Road at Monkton Road. Situated in the midst of Maryland's hunt country, this establishment offers pleasant company and surroundings. Both formal and informal settings are found indoors. This is a favorite spot for the horsey set to congregate, especially after the "point to point" steeplechases. An outside patio boasts an imaginative menu of well-prepared cuisine. $$–$$$; ☐. (410) 771–8155.

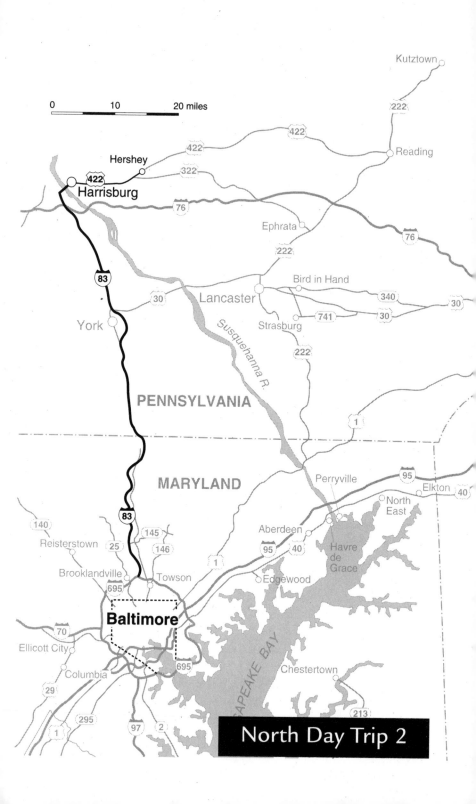

North Day Trip 2

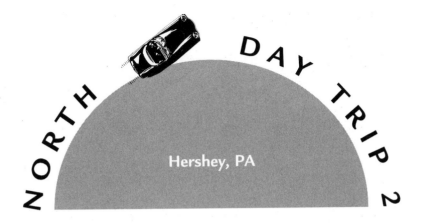

HERSHEY, PA

Chocolate lovers, beware—this place will satiate your senses! The sweet aroma pervades the town, designated the "Chocolate Capital of the World." The two main streets are—what else?—Chocolate and Cocoa Avenues, where streetlamps mimic chocolate kisses.

From Baltimore take I-83 to Harrisburg. Take US-322 east to Hershey and the attractions that nestle in the Lebanon Valley. Founded in 1903 by Milton S. Hershey, it is a planned industrial community that includes the Hershey Foods Corporation, one of the world's largest chocolate and cocoa plants.

WHAT TO SEE

Founders Hall. US-322, 1¼ miles east of P-743. On the campus of the Milton Hershey School is Founders Hall, a tribute to Mr. and Mrs. Milton Hershey. A twenty-two-minute film depicts the founding of the school. Free. (717) 520-2205.

Hershey Park. Located just off P-743 and US-422. See eighty-one acres of pure fun in the heart of chocolate country. Visitors of all ages will enjoy the full assortment of rides; serious thrill-seekers will especially like the Comet, a classic top-rated wooden roller coaster, and the Flying Falcon, a ride that gives adventurous visitors a chance to swing and twirl on a falcon's wings while 105 feet in the air. Hershey Park also presents dolphin and sea lion performances as well as a variety of daily shows, some of which feature old-time rock 'n' roll, singing and dancing from Broadway musicals, ethnic music, and Dixieland bands. A variety of food is available from the fast-food pavilions. Don't miss the chocolate-coated walkaway sundaes. Fee. For reservations call (800) 533-3131. For information call (717) HERSHEY.

ZOOAMERICA North American Wildlife Park. Adjacent to Hershey Park. This zoo offers visitors the opportunity to observe the habitats of more than 200 mammals, reptiles, fowl, and fish located in replicas of five North American regions. View black bears, snowy owls, and the endangered peregrine falcons in the North Woods, the area of the zoo representing the Canadian Everglades, or see the endangered thick-billed parrots on display in the Cactus Community, an area that represents Arizona's Sonoran Desert. Fee is included in the regular admission to Hershey Park; separate admission fee available. (717) 534-3149.

Hershey Gardens. Park Boulevard, near Hotel Hershey. A series of six themed gardens features a beautiful array of flowers, trees, and shrubs. Garden types include colonial, Italian, Japanese, English formal, and rock. Check for local information regarding the best seasons for visiting. Fee. (717) 534-3492.

Hershey Museum of American Life. Adjacent to the Hershey Park entrance at 170 Hersheypark Drive. The museum offers a colorful collection of Pennsylvania Dutch arts and crafts and rotating exhibits. Also represented are artifacts of the American Indian and Eskimo. Other exhibits include a children's discovery room, Pennsylvania-German folk art, musical instruments, baskets, pewter, and pottery. Fee. (717) 534-3439.

Hershey's Chocolate World. Park Boulevard at Hershey Park. Stroll up the ramp in this fun-filled building to see pictures and memorabilia depicting the birth of chocolate as a confection. Candy molds, milk cans, and package wrappers take you on a nostalgic trip to your sweet tooth's past. Hop aboard a moving cart to learn about chocolate—from its origin to its consumption. This is a truly delectable attraction. At the center of Chocolate World is a large indoor tropical garden that features tall stately palm trees and exotic plants that are found in the tropical regions where cocoa is harvested. Free. (717) 534-4900.

There are numerous family-oriented sites and attractions in the region, from small go-cart tracks to rail trips, caverns, and lots of outlet shopping. If you'd like to overnight in the area, you'll have no problem in finding accommodations.

To return home, take P–39 to US–322 west toward Harrisburg. Then take I–83 south to Baltimore.

WHERE TO EAT

Hotel Hershey. Park Boulevard across from Hershey Park. This lovely hotel is set within beautifully landscaped grounds. The spacious dining room offers a view of the gardens. The menu features American cuisine and is well prepared. If you overindulge, you may welcome some exercise on the adjacent biking and jogging trails. Entertainment may be featured. $$–$$$; ☐. (717) 533–2171.

Hershey Lodge and Convention Center. West Chocolate Avenue and University Drive in Hershey proper. This sprawling complex is ideal for groups as well as the individual traveler and features two dining rooms with varying fare. Quality is consistent. Lunch, $–$$; dinner, $$–$$$. ☐. (717) 533–3311.

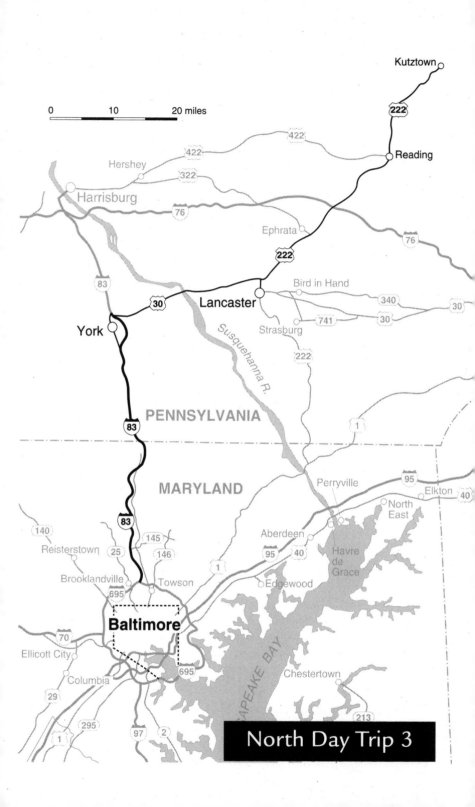

North Day Trip 3

KUTZTOWN, PA

Just an hour and a half from Baltimore, this small Pennsylvania Dutch town was founded in 1771 by George Kutz and designated the home of Pennsylvania Dutch crafts. Visitors today can observe the various techniques employed in the local art form. The biggest happening in this town is on July 4th each year. The Kutztown Folk Festival is a well-promoted event that draws enthusiastic crowds. Featured are Pennsylvania Dutch foods, arts and crafts, quilts, square dancing, and an exhibition of the Amish Plain and Fancy Dutch pageantry.

Take I-83 north out of Baltimore to York, Pennsylvania, then US-30 east out of York to Lancaster. Pick up USA-222 northeast past Reading (see Day Trip 4 in this section) and on to Kutztown.

WHERE TO GO

Crystal Cave. Two miles west of Kutztown, off US-222. The route is well marked with signs. This natural phenomenon is appropriately named for the crystalline formations found in the cavern. Fee. (610) 683-6765.

Roadside America. Between Allentown and Harrisburg, west of Kutztown at PA-22 and US-78 (exit 8), this is the nation's largest indoor miniature village. Begun more than sixty years ago by a carpenter/painter, this has become a huge indoor complex with trains, grist mill, towns, industries, and a typical Pennsylvania Dutch farm. Be certain to bring along a camera. Fee. (610) 488-6241.

LANCASTER, PA

Retrace your routing from Kutztown and head southwest on US–222 back to Lancaster. This town, rich with restored architectural heritage dating back to the early 1700s, lends itself well to a walking tour, and its history is also reflected in the colorful shops and restaurants that abound here.

During the Revolutionary War era, Lancaster was the largest city in the original thirteen colonies. It held the status of national capital for one day in 1777 and was the state capital from 1799 to 1812.

Lancaster is in the heart of Lancaster County, which is famous for its Amish and Mennonite people. Pennsylvania Dutch hospitality is well known for its traditional family recipes served abundantly in smorgasbord style. Have your day trip dinner in one of the many area restaurants boasting local fare. While the emphasis is on mealtime, it is also on snacktime! This area features pretzel making at its best. A visit to a local factory is on the agenda.

Lancaster County road signs will entertain you with such destinations as Paradise, Blue Ball, Bird-in-Hand, and Intercourse.

While tourists are eagerly recruited, it behooves the visitor to read the tourism literature offered locally to avoid infractions of area customs. In some instances photography is not welcomed, so check before snapping. For this information and more, the Pennsylvania Dutch Convention and Visitors Bureau is located east on US–30 at 501 Greenfield Road in Lancaster. An orientation to the area is presented with maps, an award-winning multi-image show "There Is a Season" that serves as an excellent orientation to the region, exhibits, brochures, and a knowledgeable counter staff. (717) 299-8901.

WHERE TO GO

Dutch Wonderland. US–30, 4 miles east of Lancaster. This forty-four-acre theme park features an overhead monorail train, which offers a bird's-eye view of its various attractions and twenty-two different rides. Traditional park activities include the exciting Log Flume ride, Stern Wheel Riverboat, Botanical Gardens, and a miniature railroad. Fee. (717) 291-1888.

Wheatland. Located at 1120 Marietta Avenue (P-23) in Lancaster. Wheatland, the mansion residence of James Buchanan, offers the visitor a unique glimpse into the life of an American president at the middle of the nineteenth century. The restored Federal-style house was built in 1828. Buchanan purchased the twenty-two-acre estate in 1848 while serving as secretary of state. At the close of Buchanan's presidency in 1861, he retired to Wheatland. Visitors can see a variety of period rooms, including the elegant American Empire dining room. Also on view are the original interior paint, grained woodwork, marble and slate mantels, columned front and rear porticoes, and other architectural details. Guided tours are available. Special Christmas candlelight tours are held in early December. Call ahead for exact dates and hours. Fee. (717) 392-8721.

Strasburg Rail Road. From Lancaster take US-222 south to P-741 and head east to Strasburg. This coal-burning, steam locomotive with coal-oil lamps and potbelly stove is well over half a century old. The train is in character with the rustic country through which it passes. The 140-year-old right-of-way of the Strasburg Rail Road winds through the very heart of Lancaster County's Amish country. Lunch and dinner are served in the dining car "Lee Brenner." If you wish, bring your picnic lunch and stop over at Groff's free Picnic Grove. Fee. (717) 687-7522.

Gast Classic Motorcars. Baby boomers who listened to the Beach Boys and Elvis will enjoy more than fifty muscle, sports, and classic cars of the '40s, '50s, and '60s at Gast Classic Motorcars, 421 Hartman Bridge Road (Route 896) in Strasburg. Bring your camera and a dose of nostalgia. Fee. (717) 687-9500.

Ephrata Cloister. From Lancaster take US-222 north to Ephrata, then go west on US-322 to Ephrata Cloister. This unique site is an eighteenth-century German Protestant monastic settlement in the Pennsylvania Dutch country. It is one of America's earliest communal societies. Housed in a unique collection of medieval-style buildings, this community of religious celibates practiced an austere lifestyle that emphasized spiritual and mystical goals rather than material objectives. Twelve of the original buildings have been restored to re-create this unusual village. Fee. Reservations needed for groups of ten or more. (717) 733-6600.

The Artworks at Doneckers. Located at 100 North State Street. This is a four-story marketplace of working artists and galleries offering a wide variety of fine arts including jewelry, pottery, collectibles, and designer crafts. Purchase your gifts directly from the artisans. Within a few blocks, you can also visit the Doneckers Community with a fashion store, restaurant, inn, and Farmers Market. Free. (717) 738-9503.

Landis Valley Museum. Located at 2451 Kissel Hill Road (take P-272 4½ miles northeast from Lancaster). The museum depicts Pennsylvania's rural heritage. Clustered around the crossroads of Landis Valley, the museum consists of a collection of twenty-two exhibit buildings and numerous objects depicting traditional crafts, skills, and lifestyles of rural Pennsylvania from the colonial era through the end of the nineteenth century. Visit the General Store. Fee. (717) 569-0401.

Bird-in-Hand Farmer's Market. Located 5 miles from Lancaster on Old Philadelphia Pike (P-340) at Maple Avenue. Visit this colorful market for fresh fruits, meats and produce, homemade baked goods, Pennsylvania Dutch pretzels and potato chips, candies, flowers and plants, jams and jellies, and homemade ice cream. Check for market days and hours. (717) 393-9674.

Plain and Fancy Farm. Continue along P-340 toward Intercourse. The Plain and Fancy Farm features a family-style eatery and the Amish Country Homestead of the Fisher family. To get a closer look at the lifestyle of the Amish, there is "The Amish Experience Theater," a high-tech and multimedia production showing the dramatic tale of an Amish family's effort to preserve a lifestyle and culture. Fee for theater. (717) 768-8400.

Heading back, take US-30 southwest out of Lancaster to York. Then take I-83 south to Baltimore.

WHERE TO EAT

Plain and Fancy Farm and Dining Room. Located 7 miles east of Lancaster on US-30 in Bird-in-Hand. Family-style Pennsylvania Dutch dining. Village of shops, buggy rides, house tours, and museums. $-$$; □. (717) 768-4400.

Willow Valley Inn and Family Restaurant. US-222, 3 miles south of Lancaster at 2416 Willow Street Pike. What began in 1943 as a Farmer's Market has grown into a full resort with lodging, shopping, and dining. Delicious farm-fresh food is served in the traditional smorgasbord style. Lodging, bake and gift shops, and an enclosed mall with twenty shops make this a good multipurpose stop. $-$$; ☐. (717) 464-2711.

Good 'n Plenty family-style eating. Take PA-896 south from US-340 at Smoketown. As the name implies, you'll get plenty of good home-cooked Penn Dutch food at this converted (and expanded) old farmhouse. A typical meal may include pork and sauerkraut, mashed potatoes, baked country sausage, baked country ham, crispy fried chicken, noodles, homemade bread, apple butter, and shoofly pie. $-$$; ☐. (717) 394-7111.

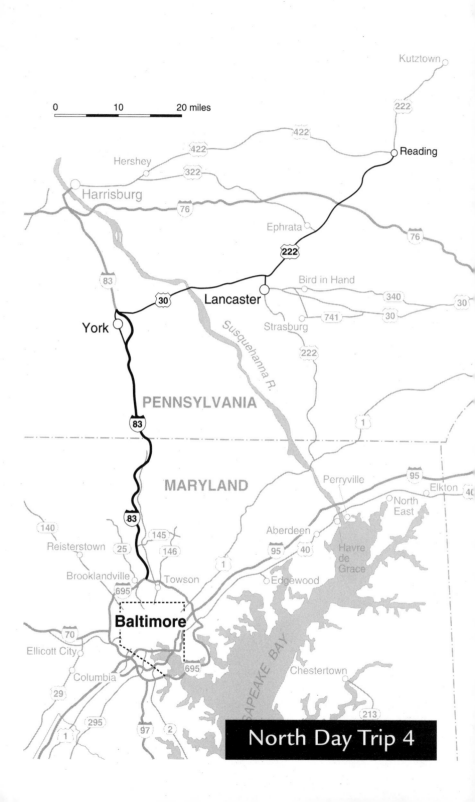

North Day Trip 4

Outlet Capital of the World:
Reading, PA

READING, PA

Forget the history—the main event in this town is in the here and now! Welcome to Reading, the "Outlet Capital of the World." Grab your mad money for some of the best bargains you'll ever find. Plan to shop for Christmas in an area saturated with more outlets for reduced-price merchandise than you can imagine. Enough said. Here's how to get there. Take I-83 north out of Baltimore to York, Pennsylvania. Pick up US-30 to Lancaster, then US-222 to Reading. For detailed maps of the area to plan a time-efficient shopping trip, write Berks County Visitors Information Association, VF Factory Outlet Complex, Park Road and Hill Avenue, Wyomissing, PA 19610. (610) 375-4085.

WHERE TO GO

The Reading Outlet Center. 800 block of North 9th Street, bounded by Douglass, Moss, and Windsor Streets. Name-brand cosmetics, linens, children's wear, sweaters, lingerie, wine and cheeses, knitted goods, and shoes. (610) 373-5495.

VF Outlet Complex. Located at 8th and Hill Avenues, West Reading-Wyomissing. Wear comfortable shoes, or buy them, as you scout bargains in this outlet paradise. A full range of famous-name clothing, handbags and luggage, power tools and accessories, china and glass, and home furnishings will place a "no holds barred" on your pocketbook. (800) 772-8336 or (610) 378-0408.

Home Furnishings and Fashion Outlet Mall. Morgantown. Take exit 22 off the Pennsylvania Turnpike. This mall features more than thirty stores, mostly selling furniture and home accessories. Some fashion. (610) 286-2000.

Outlets on Hiesters Lane. Hiesters Lane and Kutztown Road. These outlets feature the Burlington Coat Factory and Mikasa Factory stores. (610) 929-3673.

This sample of outlets will give you an indication of what to expect in this shopper's heaven. It's so extensive it can be bewildering, so write ahead for information. Reverse routing will bring you easily back to Baltimore.

WHERE TO EAT

Antique Airplane Restaurant. Located in the Dutch Colony Inn off US-422, east Mount Penn. Good food at very reasonable prices. $; ☐. (610) 779-2345.

Dempsey's Restaurant. US-222 south and P-724. Reasonable prices; often features specials. $; ☐. (610) 775-0673.

Haag's Hotel and Restaurant. Located at 3rd and Main Streets, Shartlesville, PA. Serves family-style lunches and dinners at reasonable prices. $$; ☐. (610) 488-6692.

Joe's Bistro 614. Located at 614 Penn Avenue, West Reading. Excellent cuisine. Lunch, $$-$$$; dinner, $$$; ☐. (610) 371-9966.

Shartlesville Hotel. Main Street. Offers both menu selections and family-style lunches and dinners. $-$$; no ☐. (610) 488-0260.

Day Trips from Baltimore

Travel northeast to the scenic blend of rolling farmlands and the upper Chesapeake Bay countryside. Historic paths yield glimpses of early American stone homes and mills and fields of grazing thoroughbreds. The headwaters of the bay challenge residents and visitors to the active arts of sailing and boating. Even the spectator sportsman will enjoy the bay from a well-placed lawn chair.

Spanish Jesuit missionaries visited these shores as early as 1570. Captain John Smith came here in 1608 during his visits to the head of the Chesapeake Bay and the Susquehanna River. A petition from the Upper Bay citizens in 1773 established Harford as a separate county. On March 22, 1775, in the Harford County seat of Bushtown, thirty-four prominent men penned their signatures to what is believed to be the first Declaration of Independence ever made in America by an elected body of men.

While early political events were carving a niche in history, early transportation was carving a route through the countryside. The northeast corridor saw the completion of the Baltimore & Ohio Railroad early in the nineteenth century. The Susquehanna and Tidewater Canal opened in 1839. We'll visit historic tributes to these land-and-sea feats on this day trip.

Rural life was touched by the encroaching industries of the iron furnaces, forges, and mills. Remaining structures show the architecture and artifacts of the times, while a museum of history provides a window on the rural household and way of life.

Our northeast journey will take us over the Maryland line, where we'll see a sample of neighboring Delaware. Philadelphia will be a day trip in itself. And, finally, at the outer limits of our two-hour drive, we'll venture into the historic and scenic Brandywine Valley.

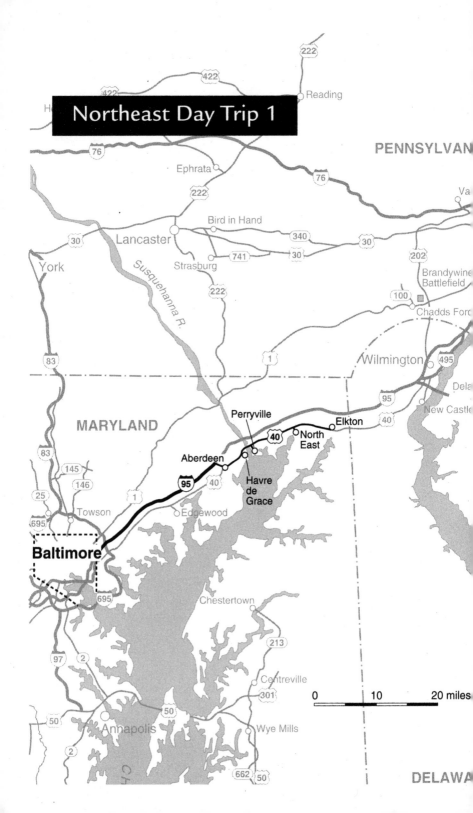

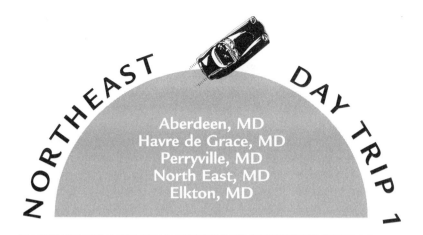

NORTHEAST DAY TRIP 1

Aberdeen, MD
Havre de Grace, MD
Perryville, MD
North East, MD
Elkton, MD

ABERDEEN, MD

Like Edgewood, this quiet country town is military-oriented and is the home of many of the civilian employees of the nearby Proving Ground. It is host to the U.S. Army Ordnance Museum—a site of considerable value to visitors interested in the history of military weaponry. Continue on I-95 north to M-22 and head east to Aberdeen.

WHERE TO GO

Aberdeen Proving Ground. From Aberdeen, continue on M-22 east to the entrance of the Proving Ground. This road is also known as the Aberdeen Thruway and becomes the Northern Thruway as it enters the Proving Ground. Pick up your visitor information at the main gate of this 80,000-acre reservation. Constructed in 1917, it was used for the development and testing of artillery. A display of U.S. tanks at the entrance of the grounds includes models beginning with 1918.

The U.S. Army Ordnance Museum. Located on the property of the Aberdeen Proving Ground, this museum presents the most comprehensive collection of small arms, artillery, combat vehicles, and ammunition in the country. Among the items on display are body armor, uniforms, weapons of historic importance (Gatling Gun and German V2 Rocket), General Pershing's Locomobile, and the "Tank Park," featuring an array of vehicles ranging from World War I through Desert Storm. Free. (410) 278-3602.

HAVRE DE GRACE, MD

This delightfully scenic town was settled before the Revolutionary War. Located at the headwaters of the Chesapeake Bay where it meets the Susquehanna River, its history is a rich one. In 1791, it narrowly lost out to Washington, DC, as the site of the nation's capital. The town enjoyed significant commerce in coal, lumber, grain, ore, and iron products through its canal between Havre de Grace and Pennsylvania. In 1836 a railroad and a steamship line were added. While the War of 1812 devastated many of its buildings, some examples of the architectural styles erected by the wealthy merchants of the 1880s remain and are maintained as homes or offices today. The current City Hall on Union Avenue was once a three-story opera house and was damaged by fire in 1920. It was later reconstructed as the present two-story building. Take I-95 north to exit 89 east, M-155 east to Havre de Grace.

WHERE TO GO

Tydings Memorial Park. Commerce Street and Union Avenue. This peaceful plot of green marks the spot where British troops landed in 1813 to sack and burn the town. It is the site of the Annual Harford Seafood Festival and the Arts and Crafts Fair.

The Concord Point Lighthouse. Lafayette Street near Tydings Memorial Park. Considered among the oldest of such structures on the East Coast, the lighthouse was erected in 1829 and was continuously operated until 1976. It offers today's visitors a magnificent view of the bay. Free. The **John O'Neill Monument** and a citizens monument to the memory of all the soldiers who fought in World War I are located here.

The Susquehanna Museum of Havre de Grace. Conesteo Street. The museum, situated at the remains of the first lock of the Susquehanna and Tidewater Canal, is furnished in the manner of an 1840s lockhouse. Housing artifacts significant to waterways, it also features a tivet bridge over a lock that was used to get to the other side of the canal. Fee. Reservations for groups are recommended. (410) 939-5780.

The Havre de Grace Decoy Museum. 215 Giles Street. This museum supports a long-standing tradition of hand-carved decoys and features complete collections of Madison Mitchell and Paul Gibson. Fee. (410) 939-3739.

Rock Run Mill. From Havre de Grace take M-155 west to Lapidum Road, crossing over I-95. At Lapidum Road turn right. Take this directly into Susquehanna State Park (see listing at back of book). This stone mill was built in 1794 and boasts a twelve-ton water wheel, which still grinds corn today. This area was a major crossroads from Philadelphia during the nineteenth century. Also on the park grounds is the **Jersey Toll House** (c. 1818), which was the residence of the toll keeper for Rock Run. Currently it houses mementos of the past and an environmental display demonstrating watershed protection. Fee. (410) 939-0643.

The Steppingstone Museum. Located at 463 Quaker Bottom Road in Susquehanna State Park (see listing in back of book). Surrounded by barns and other farm buildings, this stone farmhouse contains exhibits and displays more than 13,000 pieces of rural "Americana" between 1880 and 1910. The farmhouse is arranged as a country house with rear terrace overlooking the Susquehanna River. The tools of a woodworker, leather worker, blacksmith, and other artisans are on display. Fee. (410) 939-2299.

The Susquehanna Trading Co. Located at 324 North Union Avenue. This shop claims the largest collection of decoys on the East Coast and specializes in working decoys of the Chesapeake Bay region. Free. (410) 939-4252.

WHERE TO EAT

The Bayou. Located at 927 Pulaski Highway (US-40). Located in Havre de Grace, this restaurant offers a well-rounded menu of American cuisine and excellent lunches. $-$$; ☐. (410) 939-3565.

MacGregor's Restaurant and Tavern. Located at 331 St. John Street. Originally an 1860 grainmill and then remodeled as a bank in 1924, this restaurant features American cuisine and specializes in local seafood dishes. Visitors also enjoy a magnificent view of the Susquehanna River. $-$$; ☐. (410) 939-3003.

Tidewater Grill. At the foot of Franklin Street in Havre de Grace. Located on the water, this favorite dining spot features an excellent seafood selection and a pleasant view of the Susquehanna River. Lunch, $$; dinner, $$$; ☐. (410) 939-3313 or (410) 575-7045.

PERRYVILLE, MD

Perryville is located in Cecil County near the top of the Chesapeake Bay. It is well placed in an area of gently rolling hills and scenic rivers. Various mansions, taverns, mills, and inns easily take the visitor back to colonial times. Drive out of Havre de Grace on US-40 north across the Susquehanna Toll Bridge. Take M-222 southeast to M-7 and then northeast to Perryville.

WHERE TO GO

Horizon Outlet Center at Perryville. Exit 93 off I-95 takes you to Perryville's shopping haven. All types of factory-outlet stores are here—Nike, Mikasa, and Geoffrey Beene are just three of forty-seven stores. Free parking. (800) 866-5900.

The Zoo at Plumpton Park. 1416 Telegraph Road. Exit 100 off I-95 to M-272 north will take you to this family-friendly zoo with picnic area and playground. Quiet nature trails and more than 250 animals to visit. Fee. (410) 658-6850.

NORTH EAST, MD

Settlement in this area seems to have originally centered on a flour mill erected here in 1716. Also in operation here was a forge erected around 1735 by the Principio Company. The buildings in existence today are largely from the late nineteenth and early twentieth centuries. Several small cottage industries are sustained by this community today. Continue on M-7 northeast to North East.

WHERE TO GO

St. Mary Anne's Protestant Episcopal Church. South Main Street (M-272). Erected in 1742, this church is one of the oldest in Cecil County. The structure is gambrel-roofed with clipped gables and round-headed windows. The brick is laid in Flemish bond style. The cornerstone bears the initials of the rector and vestrymen. A Bible, communion vessels, and a Book of Common Prayer presented by Queen Elizabeth II are still used in special services. The graveyard contains the markers of some American Indian converts. Fee. Open daily; no phone.

The Upper Bay Museum. In North East, take M–272 south to Walnut Street. Turn right and proceed to the North East Community Park. This exhibit brings the taste and history of the upper Chesapeake Bay to its visitors. Fishing, boating, and hunting artifacts, native to this area, are on display. Open 10:00 A.M. to 4:00 P.M. Saturday and Sunday; other hours vary. Call to schedule a tour. Free; donations accepted. (410) 287–0672.

ELKTON, MD

This county seat was known in colonial days as "Head of Elk." It occupies an important page in American history as the point where troops and supplies of both armies were shifted from time to time during the Revolutionary War. At **Hollingsworth Tavern** on Main Street, the commanding British general, Lord Howe, may not have been impressed that, on the previous night, General George Washington had slept in the very room prepared for Howe.

The town is noted as an early shipping point for the wheat raised in the rich Piedmont area. Surrounding creeks supplied the waterpower for small paper and textile factories that were built in the early nineteenth century.

Perhaps one of its most unique "industries" was the lucrative business of marrying couples who were unwilling to wait the time required in surrounding states. While a forty-eight-hour waiting period was finally adopted in 1938 by Maryland, the town still has its wedding chapels (Wedding Chapel, 142 East Main Street, Elkton, 410–398–3640) and remains a popular place for elopements. Depart North East on M–272 north to US–40 to Elkton. For further information on Elkton or Cecil County, including fairs and events, call (800) CECIL-95.

WHERE TO GO

Historical Society Museum. Located at 135 East Main Street. Exhibits include an early kitchen with utensils, country store, firehouse, and school room. Call for hours. (410) 398–1790.

The Mitchell House. Located next to the library, it was built in 1769 and was the home of Dr. Abraham Mitchell, a noted physician.

It served as a hospital for wounded Continental soldiers who were under Dr. Mitchell's care during the Revolution. The structure is of stuccoed brick and is maintained as a private home (drive-by only).

Mount Harmon Plantation. From Elkton take M–213 south to M–282 west and follow the signs. This eighteenth-century tobacco plantation features a restored mansion, beautiful grounds, and formal boxwood gardens. It rests elegantly on the shores of the Sassafras River and is open for tours from April through October. Fee. (410) 275–8819.

WILMINGTON, DE

"Chemical Capital of the World" as well as industrial and shipping hub, Wilmington has established itself as the largest city in Delaware. It was initially known as Fort Christina in 1638 and later renamed when wealthy Quakers laid out the present town in 1731. It grew into an important market and shipping center, assisted by its accessibility to other eastern ports and the abundant waterpower in the Brandywine River Valley.

A major benefactor arrived on the scene in the early nineteenth century. Eleuthere du Pont de Nemours established a high-quality gunpowder manufacturing industry here and was instrumental in bringing to this city the leading industrial status it enjoys today. The Du Pont Corporation has grown to be one of the largest industrial establishments in the world.

From Baltimore you can take I-95 directly to Wilmington, or take your time and wend your way along the route proposed in Day Trip 1 of this sector.

WHERE TO GO

Delaware Museum of Natural History. Centerville, Delaware, 5 miles northwest of Wilmington. From I-95 north, take exit 6 to D-52. Take D-52 north for 4 miles. Experience nature from the wilds of Africa to the quiet restfulness of the local area in dioramas, exhibits, special programs, and the interactive discovery room where

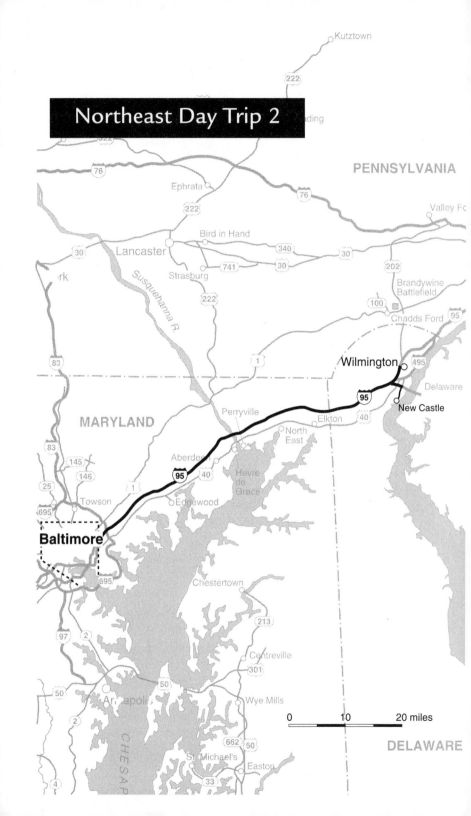

Northeast Day Trip 2

learning is great fun. The exhibit highlights include a walk over the Great Barrier Reef, exotic birds and shells—including a 500-pound clam—and dinosaurs. There are also films on a variety of natural history subjects. Fee. (302) 658-9111.

The Hagley Museum. From I-95 in Wilmington, take D-52 northwest to D-141 east for ½ mile. The original Du Pont Company's black powder mills are now the site of the 225-acre complex of the Hagley Museum, located along the Brandywine River. It offers a unique glimpse into American industrial life in the nineteenth century. The main building houses exhibits that trace America's industrial development from colonial water-powered flour mills to the giant steam-powered industries of the late nineteenth century. Leaving the main museum building, you will enter the powder yards where massive granite mills are a testimony to the age of waterpower and the powderman makes his routine rounds of demonstrations. Fee. (302) 658-2400.

The original du Pont home, **Eleutherian Mills,** on the museum grounds, is filled with the heirlooms of five generations. A barn filled with carriages and wagons, a garden, and the surrounding grounds are open to explore. Built in 1803, this charming Georgian-style residence artfully reflects the tastes of the family and the era. It is located ¼ mile from the main exhibit building and may be reached by a small bus. (Same fee and phone as above.)

Delaware History Museum. Located ½ mile off I-95 and five blocks from the Amtrak station, the museum houses changing self-guided exhibits in a renovated 1940s Art Deco–style Woolworth's. Guided tours and programs available by appointment for visitors of all ages. The permanent exhibit "Distinctly Delaware" is slated to open in December 1998. Adjoining gift shop with Delaware memorabilia. Rooms and galleries are also available for receptions, conferences, and meetings. The museum is part of the Delaware History Center complex on Market Street Mall. Free. (302) 655-7161.

The Delaware Art Museum. Located at 2301 Kentmere Parkway in Wilmington. Take D-52 north off I-95 to the museum, which houses one of the country's finest collections of American paintings, sculpture, photographs, and crafts. Various changing exhibitions of traditional and contemporary arts, plus a children's gallery for an enjoyable hands-on encounter with art, make this a valuable stop for the whole family. Fee; call for "free" hours. (302) 571-9590.

Old Town Hall. Located ½ mile off I-95 and five blocks from the Amtrak station. This Georgian-style structure was built between 1798 and 1800 and functioned as a center of political and social activities during the height of Wilmington's mercantile-milling economy. Now a museum, it houses changing exhibits that focus on a specific event from its past. Located next to the Delaware History Museum and gift shop; near major hotels and restaurants. Part of the Delaware History Center complex on Market Street Mall. Free. (302) 655-7161.

Willingtown Square. Located ½ mile off I-95 and five blocks from the Amtrak station. Composed of late eighteenth- and early-nineteenth-century homes currently used for meeting rooms and office space, which border a grass area good for picnic lunches. The square is named for Thomas Willing, who in 1731 laid out the village that was to become Wilmington. Part of the Delaware History Center complex on Market Street Mall, which also includes the Delaware History Museum, gift shop, and Old Town Hall. Free (302) 655-7161.

The Grand Opera House. Located at 818 Market Street Mall. Built by the Masons of Delaware in 1871, this fine example of cast-iron architecture is Delaware's Center for the Performing Arts. The opera house is a National Historic Landmark and featured such famous performers as Ethel Barrymore, Edwin Booth, George M. Cohan, and Buffalo Bill Cody. Live performances (fee) and special dinners and receptions are held in the elegant decor of the Victorian era. Year-round programs featuring the Delaware Symphony and Opera Delaware are also held here. Free tours. (302) 658-7898.

Nemours Mansion. Rockland Road between US-202 and D-141. The mansion is a fine example of a modified Louis XVI chateau. Designed by Carrere and Hastings of New York, it was built between 1909 and 1910 by Smyth and Son of Wilmington for Alfred I. du Pont, a member of the American manufacturing family. Containing seventy-seven rooms, the house is furnished with fine examples of antique furniture, rare rugs, tapestries, and outstanding artwork.

The gardens, extending ⅓ mile along the main vista of the house, were influenced greatly by Mr. du Pont's many trips to Europe and are a fine example of a classic French-style design. Visitors must be older than sixteen years of age and must be able to negotiate stairways; photographs are not permitted in the mansion. Tours take a minimum of two hours. Fee. (302) 651–6912.

Rockwood. Located at 610 Shipley Road. Inspired by an English country house, this fine example of Rural Gothic architecture reflects the lifestyle of several generations of Wilmington businessmen. Built in 1851 by Joseph Shipley, a Quaker merchant, the estate passed down through his family. The museum contains decorative arts and archives ranging from the seventeenth to the early twentieth centuries and includes American, European, and Oriental objects. Fee. (302) 761–4340.

Winterthur Museum and Gardens. From Wilmington take exit 7 off I-95 to D-52 northwest for 6 miles. This vast museum in a 963-acre country setting is the extraordinary legacy of Henry Francis du Pont. A collection of more than 70,000 objects is housed in a nine-story sprawling building set among 200 landscaped acres, rolling meadows, and untouched woods. Prepare to witness an absolutely exquisite collection of American antiques and a garden of native and exotic plants of spectacular beauty. Fee. (302) 888–4600; (800) 448–3883.

Wilmington & Western Railroad. Greenbank Station, Newport-Gap Pike. Take D-41 ¼ mile north to intersection with Kirkwood Highway, D-2. Travel aboard vintage steam trains through the famous Red Clay Valley. Operates April through December. Fee. (302) 998–1930.

WHERE TO EAT

Harry's Savoy Grill. Located at 2020 Naaman's Road (Route 92), North Wilmington. Features gas lamps, live piano, strolling magicians, and crackling fireplaces. An elegant dining experience with attentive service and an interesting, varied menu. $$–$$$; ☐. (302) 475–3000.

Hotel du Pont's Brandywine and Green Room. Hotel du Pont, 11th and Market Streets. Consistently good food and competent service. Ornately decorated; dress code observed. Children's menu available. Lunch, $$–$$$; dinner, $$$; ☐. Brandywine, (302) 594–3156; Green Room, (302) 594–3154.

NEW CASTLE, DE

Since 1651, New Castle has nestled on the banks of the Delaware River. Its history is as engaging as its cobblestone streets. Founded by the Dutch, conquered by the Swedes and English, and prominent as the capital of Delaware in the early Revolutionary War era, New Castle began her story when European explorers sailed up the Delaware. In 1682, William Penn came ashore here and took possession, but the counties that were already well established became quickly dissatisfied with his rule. In 1704, he granted them a separate legislature and New Castle became the colonial capital of Delaware. Many of the private, restored homes around the green and along The Strand are especially representative of the beauty of the architecture in the area. From Wilmington take D-9 south to New Castle. New Castle Visitors Bureau, (302) 652–4088.

WHERE TO GO

The George Reed II House. Located at 42 The Strand. The Historic Society of Delaware maintains this fine example of late Georgian architecture overlooking the Delaware River. The formal garden surrounding the house was completed in 1874 and remains faithful to its original design. Fee. (302) 322–8411.

The Green. Delaware Street between Third and Market Streets. This area was laid out in 1655 by Peter Stuyvesant, the Dutch colonial governor and founder of New York. It served as the center for fairs and weekly markets. It was also the site of the high sheriff's house, with an adjoining jail. In the jail yard a high stone wall encloses a pillory, gallows, and whipping post. Free.

The Strand. This interesting cobblestone street near the river is charmingly bordered by shady brick walks and brick gutters. Fine town houses that date back to 1679, survivors of the "Great Fire" of 1824, line The Strand.

The New Castle Court House. Delaware Street between Third and Market Streets. Erected in 1732, it served as Delaware's colonial capitol and first statehouse. It was restored in 1804 to its original appearance, as in a drawing by Benjamin Henry Latrobe. Free. (302) 323–4453.

The Old Dutch House. 32 North Third Street. This house, thought to be the oldest brick house in the state, was built in the late seventeenth century. Restored as a museum, it displays household utensils of the early Dutch settlers. Fee. (302) 322-9168.

WHERE TO EAT

Arsenal on the Green. 30 Market Street. American Continental cuisine. Casual elegance in a warm colonial atmosphere. Extensive wine list. $$$; ☐. (302) 328-1290.

Casablanca. 4010 North Du Pont Highway, New Castle. Serving Moroccan and Middle Eastern foods, this is more than a restaurant—it's a pleasant trip to an exotic land. $$; ☐. (302) 652-5344.

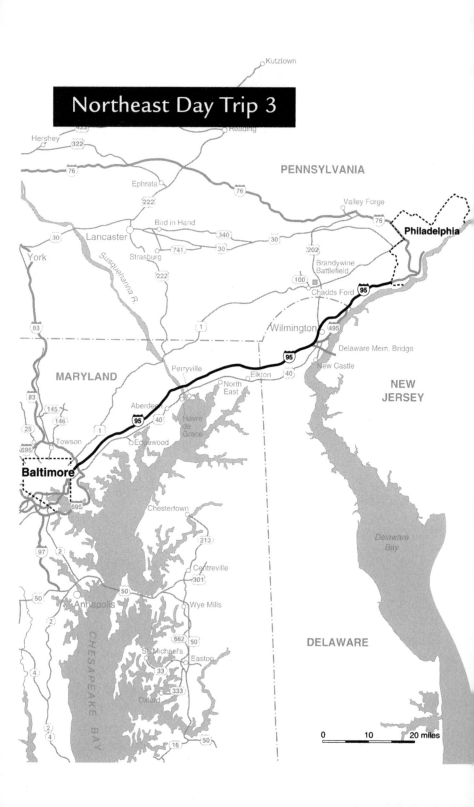

Northeast Day Trip 3

Philadelphia, PA

PHILADELPHIA, PA

Philadelphia is a day trip unto itself. It's a journey into the nation's past, tracing the footsteps of George Washington, Benjamin Franklin, and Thomas Jefferson through Independence National Historical Park. Get in touch with the enthusiasm and commitment of our fore-fathers as you touch the Liberty Bell and stand in the room where the Declaration of Independence and the U.S. Constitution were signed.

World-class museums of art, science, and history will draw you into their quiet environs and fill your day with their wonders. The performing arts—drama, music, ballet, and opera—will easily fill your evening. The culinary arts are practiced in a virtual restaurant renaissance known globally for fine quality. While at least one visit to Old Bookbinder's Restaurant is a must, many Philadelphia restaurants boast more personalized service and excellent food. And, if you plan to stay overnight, be sure to sample the many opportunities for nightlife—Philadelphia style.

Philadelphia is also a day trip into the present. It is a beautiful city in touch with the times. Clean, tastefully forested streets border city blocks of impressive buildings. Fine shops and fun stores offer the visitor unending opportunities to make just the right purchase. The city is friendly and logically designed, making it excellent for a walking tour. Some of the sights that should not be missed include the Philadelphia Museum of Art, Independence National Historical Park, Independence Hall, the Liberty Bell, Betsy Ross House, and the Franklin Mint Museum.

Whatever your interests might be as you approach Philadelphia for your day trip, your first stop should be the visitor center at Third and Chestnut Streets in the heart of the historic district. Here you can learn about daily programs and activities and see the introductory film "Independence," which was directed by John Huston. Some free tickets for nearby attractions and information about facilities for the disabled and foreign language services are available at the visitor center.

Philadelphia offers such a wealth of sights and activities that detailed listings are impossible to include here. Suffice it to say that this wonderful destination exists within a day trip from Baltimore. Take I-95 north from Baltimore to Philadelphia.

You may find it wise to write in advance for information so that your travels will be time-efficient and focused on your specific interests. It is a big city, and a map of the area, especially the historic district, will be most helpful. Contact the Philadelphia Convention and Visitors Bureau, 1515 Market Street, Suite 2020, Philadelphia, PA 19102. (215) 636-1666 or (800) 537-7676.

NORTHEAST DAY TRIP 4

The Brandywine Valley, PA
Worth More Time:
Valley Forge National
Historical Park, PA

THE BRANDYWINE VALLEY, PA

Rich with culture, the Brandywine Valley has become synonymous with regional art. The artists and craftsmen of the area were, and are still, some of the finest in our country. Examples of their work can be found in many historic inns, antiques shops, and museums dotting the valley.

A visit to this area is a step back into America's past. This charming countryside along the banks of the Brandywine River features museums, country estates, and some of our country's finest natural, historic, and artistic treasures. Take I-95 northeast to Wilmington, Delaware, and then the US-202 north exit to the Brandywine Valley.

WHERE TO GO

Brandywine Battlefield State Park. Take US-202 north to US-1 west to Chadds Ford. Visit the information center here to see dioramas and audiovisual presentations depicting the story of General George Washington's defeat by the British at the Battle of Brandywine in 1777. Two historic houses within the park, Washington's headquarters and the Marquis de LaFayette's quarters, show the life and times of the Revolutionary War period. Fee. (610) 459-3342.

Brandywine River Museum and Native Plants Garden. Continue west on US-1 in Chadds Ford to the P-100 junction. Housed in a restored Civl War-era grist mill is an unparalleled collection of art by the Wyeth family and other nineteenth- and twentieth-century American artists. Special focus is on works representing the artistic heritage

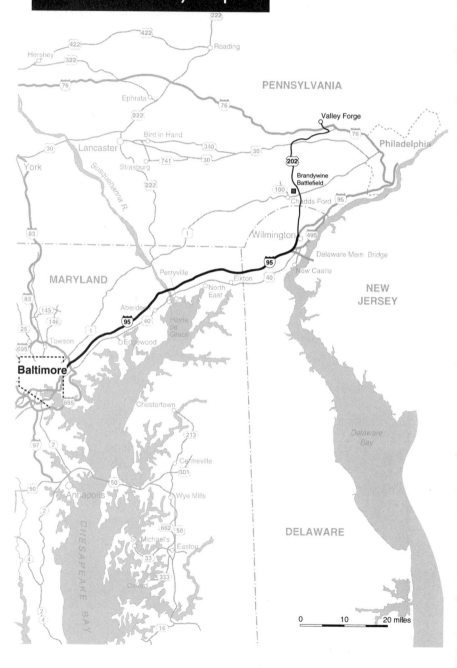

Northeast Day Trip 4

Hershey

Reading

422
322
222
76

PENNSYLVANIA

Ephrata

76

222

Bird in Hand

Lancaster

340

30

Valley Forge

202

76

Philadelphia

York

30

741

30

Strasburg

100

Brandywine
Battlefield

83

222

Susquehanna R.

1

Chadds Ford

95

Wilmington

495

MARYLAND

Perryville

North
East

Elkton

40

Delaware Mem. Bridge

New Castle

NEW
JERSEY

83

145

146

Aberdeen

Havre
de
Grace

95

40

25

Towson

1

Edgewood

695

Baltimore

695

Chestertown

213

Delaware
Bay

97

2

Centreville

301

50

Annapolis

Wye Mills

2

662

50

DELAWARE

St. Michael's

Easton

33

4

333

2
4

C H E S A P E A K E   B A Y

16

0   10   20 miles

of the Brandywine Valley. The museum is in an ideal setting, nestled on the peaceful green banks overlooking the river. Special exhibitions are held throughout the year in addition to permanent ones. Wildflower gardens, featuring plants native to the Brandywine Valley, surround the museum. Gardens free. Museum fee. (610) 388-2700.

Longwood Gardens. Continue west to Kennett Square. This lovely horticultural showplace was developed by Pierre S. du Pont as a country estate. Longwood Gardens covers more than 700 acres of flowing lawns accented with fountains and sculpture. A four-acre indoor conservatory is open year-round. Special seasonal displays are coupled with permanent exhibits of exotic plants from around the world. A tourist information center is on the premises. Fee. (610) 388-1000.

Phillips Mushroom Place. Continue along US-1 west in Kennett Square. Known as the "World's Mushroom Capital," Phillips houses a mushroom museum that explains the history, lore, and mystique of mushrooms through a motion picture, dioramas, slide presentations, and exhibits. Here the visitor observes growing mushrooms in all stages of their development. The adjoining **Market Place** offers a selection of imported gourmet foods with an offering of homemade soups, sandwiches, and, of course, mushroom specialties. Fee. (610) 388-6082.

Chadds Ford Winery. Take a wine-tasting tour by returning to Chadds Ford via US-1 east. The winery is located between the Brandywine Battlefield State Park and Longwood Gardens. Free tours and tastings are offered during winery hours, with retail sales on the premises. (610) 388-6221.

If your schedule permits, return routing to Baltimore may be planned via US-1 south through the scenic upper Chesapeake Bay territories of Cecil County and the beautiful farmlands of Harford County. For a more fast-track return, take US-202 south out of Chadds Ford to Wilmington, Delaware, and pick up I-95 south to Baltimore.

WORTH MORE TIME

VALLEY FORGE NATIONAL HISTORICAL PARK, PA

The 3,600-acre park is the site of the famed winter encampment of General George Washington and the Continental Army in the unforgiving winter of 1777 to 1778. Restored buildings, soldiers' huts, cannon emplacements, and the natural setting help re-create the turning point of the American Revolution. Pack your bike, your picnic, or your hiking shoes to take extra advantage of this visitors' delight. There is a 5-mile marked biking and hiking trail within the park. Adjacent to the area are the **Washington Memorial Chapel,** the **National Carillon,** the **Museum of the Valley Forge Historical Society,** and **Washington's headquarters.** Fee. (610) 783–1077.

Take US-202/322 northeast out of Chadds Ford to exit 2A (P-252). Also designated Valley Forge Road, this routing will take you directly to the historical park. This destination is beyond the recommended two-hour perimeter, but its value for buffs of American history makes it an exception.

WHERE TO GO

Mill Grove. Audubon Road at Pawlings Road. Take US-202 north to US-422 west. Turn right onto P-363 and left onto Audubon Road. This museum and wildlife sanctuary was owned in 1784 by Jean Audubon, the father of artist, naturalist, and author John James Audubon. This mansion now displays Audubon's major artistic works as well as murals by George M. Harding, which portray Audubon's adventures and scenes of bird life. More than 175 species of birds and 400 species of flowering plants have been identified in the sanctuary. Free, donations accepted. (610) 666–5593.

The Wharton Esherick Museum. Horseshoe Trail. Take US-202 north to P-252 (Paoli). After about 40 miles, turn right onto Diamond Rock Road and follow signs to the museum. Wharton Esherick was a prominent American artist, best known for his sculptural furniture and furnishings for which he has been called the dean of American craftsmen. This museum was once his studio, which he spent forty years building and enlarging. Visitors can view Esherick's work by entering the studio and observing the carved doors and the sculpted heater grilles and light switches. There are also more than 200 paintings, woodcuts, prints, sculpture in wood, stone and ceramic, and furniture and utensils that were produced by the artist between 1920 and 1970. Guided tours are available; reservations are required. Fee. (610) 644–5822.

WHERE TO EAT

Hank's Place Homestyle Cooking. Junction US-1 at P-100 (across from the Brandywine River Museum). Old-fashioned breakfasts, luncheons, and early dinners are served here. The restaurant is open from 5:00 A.M. to 7:00 P.M. The breakfasts were critically acclaimed by *Gourmet* magazine. $-$$, no ☐. (610) 388-7061.

The Kennedy-Supplee Restaurant. Located at 1100 West Valley Forge Road P-23, right in Valley Forge National Park. Sumptuous American cuisine served in the elegant atmosphere of a nineteenth-century mansion. Enjoy full course entrees in one of seven beautiful dining rooms. Open for lunch Monday-Friday and dinner Monday-Saturday. Closed Sundays. $$$; ☐. (610) 337-3777.

Day Trips from Baltimore

Travel southeast to tour the heartland of Maryland's romantic and political past. Queen Anne's County was named for England's eighteenth-century ruler, and its courthouse at Centreville is Maryland's oldest in continuous use. Queen Anne's gives way to Talbot County and the home of the official state tree—the Wye Oak. Nearby Wye Mills was used to grind flour for General Washington's troops during the American Revolution.

Maryland's Eastern Shore, where the Chesapeake Bay is a part of the scenario of life, was the setting of James A. Michener's novel *Chesapeake*. These scenic flatlands provide bike routes ad infinitum. Bikers will enjoy the easy pedaling and stimulating sights of the southeast.

In the cemeteries here, headstones tell the stories of Revolutionary War patriots. You'll discover country stores and curiosity shops full of rustic souvenirs, as well as blocks of appealing homes that lead to the slips and docks harboring boats and seafood restaurants.

Oxford and St. Michaels, both historic seaport towns in Talbot County, are deeply rooted in the nation's early history. Easton, the "Colonial Capital of the Eastern Shore," is one of the cultural centers of the Shore. The annual Waterfowl Festival held here is a not-to-be-missed display of decoy carving, an indigenous art.

Beyond Easton, Oxford, and St. Michaels, the Shore is a patchwork quilt of picturesque towns surrounded by fields of corn, potatoes, soybeans, and tomatoes. In summer, fresh produce stands abound on many of the area's traveling routes. Don't miss the experience of biting into a Maryland tomato. It will absolutely spoil you for pale imitations grown elsewhere. And don't husk the corn! Soak it in water and roast it in the oven or on coals for the outstanding flavor of "Silver Queen Corn." The pièce de résistance of your visit to the Shore is the fine traditional fare found in its proud inns and restaurants. Summer menus feature crabs and fresh fish, while in autumn and winter, oysters and clams are the catch of the day.

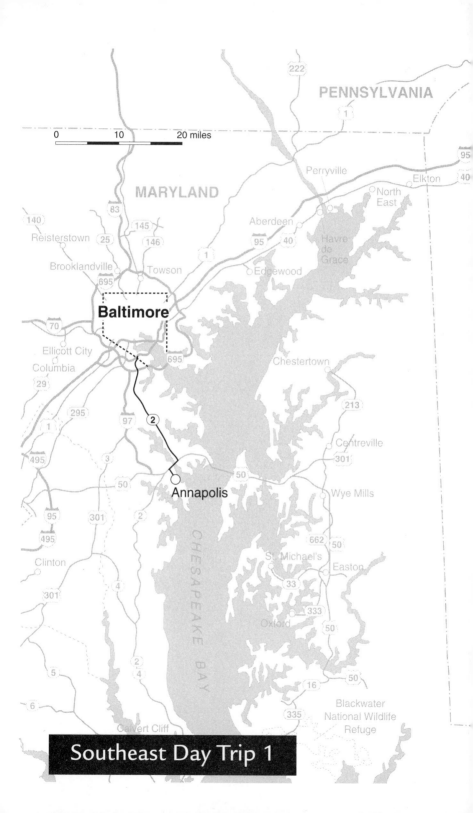

Southeast Day Trip 1

ANNAPOLIS, MD

Put on comfortable walking shoes, pack some stale bread for the ducks, and prepare to commune with history for your walking tour on the cobblestone streets of Annapolis.

Originating in 1649, Annapolis has been aptly dubbed "the museum without walls." Streets here are reminiscent of our nation's British beginnings, with names such as Duke of Gloucester, Prince George, Cornhill, King George, and Fleet. Colonial mansions and nineteenth-century town houses line the quaint walkways.

Annapolis was among the first American cities to develop within a pattern, rather than by chance. Consequently, the two main circles, State and Church, provide the hubs from which the secondary streets radiate. In the center of Church Circle stands **St. Anne's** with its impressive spire, and in the center of State Circle stands the **State House** of Maryland—two worthy sites to visit on the walking tour.

In the pre-Revolutionary days, Annapolis was the favorite child of the social as well as the political set. This colonial, cosmopolitan community was the center of gala parties, sporting events, balls, and theatricals. You'll see this social flair reflected in the gracious homes, renowned as some of the finest Georgian architecture in North America.

The town and the harbor have treated each other well over the centuries. A mutual respect is evident. The commerce that water brings is cultivated like a prime crop. The fruits of the Chesapeake Bay are offered fresh from bushel baskets or prepared from traditional recipes. Pleasure craft dot the harbor and slip in and out of manicured marinas. The Spa Creek drawbridge goes up to allow these white beauties with billowing sails to glide past.

While space does not permit detailing all there is to do in Annapolis, the following is an overview of the activities that keep most people busy on this day trip. Good shopping opportunities are everywhere. Creative pottery, crafts, home decorations, and clothing are among the choice purchases. Souvenirs abound. Several places offer excellent varieties of ice cream, and a Main Street shop features thick slices of fudge made right before your very eyes (and nose). The gulls, ducks, and assorted birds will keep you busy at the City Dock if you bring your bread and crackers. A water tour is also offered at the foot of City Dock.

From Baltimore take M-295 south (Baltimore-Washington Expressway) to I-695 east. Then pick up M-3 south to I-97 south to

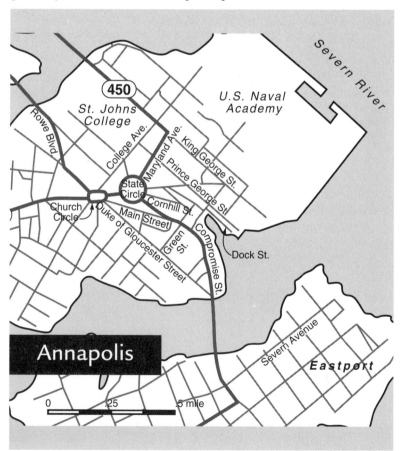

U.S.–50 east and exit at Rowe Boulevard into State Circle, Annapolis. Drive carefully, as the road is well patrolled with unmarked vehicles.

WHERE TO GO

U.S. Naval Academy. King George Street. Established in 1845, this expansive monument to higher learning is a Registered National Historic Landmark. The 329-acre campus is conducive to strolling or biking and offers a seawall view of the academy yawls in their tutored maneuvers. "Mother Bancroft" is the name lovingly given to **Bancroft Hall** by the 4,500 midshipmen who dwell in this home-away-from-home. Impeccable order in the dormitory sets the standard that prevails from ship to shore.

   The Naval Academy Chapel. Dominating the campus, this impressive structure is adorned with magnificent stained-glass windows and massive bronze doors. The traditional singing of the Navy Hymn, "Eternal Father Strong to Save," at the conclusion of services is an experience long remembered by visitors. Each spring the chapel becomes especially alive with Commissioning Week weddings. In the crypt beneath the chapel is the bronze and marble **Sarcophagus of John Paul Jones,** the naval hero of the American Revolution. The **USNA Museum** in Preble Hall contains paintings of naval heroes, ship models, uniforms, and naval memorabilia. The precision Dress Parades are always a treat to see. Stop in the information center located in Ricketts Hall for specific information and a map of the grounds. Charge for guide service only. (410) 263–6933.

   Chesapeake Marine Tours. Slip 20, City Dock. Tour Annapolis with a water view perspective. A series of tours ranging from forty minutes to a full "Day on the Bay" offers narrated excursions complete with comforts and refreshments. There are also cruises to Maryland's Eastern Shore, across the Chesapeake Bay. Fee. (410) 268–7600.

   Market House. Located at the head of City Dock, Market House is filled with stalls featuring fresh produce, fancy cheeses, breads and pastries, stand-up eating spots, and, of course, fresh seafood. Bring your cooler along to take home some of this Chesapeake bounty. On the sidewalk at the head of the City Dock, look for the plaque commemorating the 1767 arrival of Kunta Kinte, immortalized by Alex Haley in Roots.

Historic Annapolis Foundation Museum Store. Located at 77 Main Street, between Compromise and Greens Streets, this building was constructed in 1810 and served as a commissary that provided food to the Continental Army during the Revolutionary War. Here, you can rent a self-guided walking audiocassette tour of the historic district, narrated by Walter Cronkite. Fee. (410) 268-5576.

Cornhill Street. From Market House, take Cornhill Street to State Circle. Along the way you'll see town houses reminiscent of the colonial era. The street boasts fine examples of restored old homes that abound in this historic district. Door decorations are especially delightful at Christmastime.

Maryland State House. State Circle. Completed in 1698, this is the oldest statehouse in continuous legislative use in the nation. This Registered National Historic Landmark occupies a picture postcard setting atop an elevated crest. It was the national capitol between November 1783 and August 1784 and was the site of the ratification of the Treaty of Paris, as well as where George Washington resigned his commission as Commander-in-Chief of the Continental Armies. On the surrounding grounds, visitors can see the cannon that arrived on the *Ark* and the *Dove* along with many original settlers in Maryland in 1634. The tiny brick Treasury building stands as the oldest public building in the state. An audiovisual program and guided tours are available at the State House Visitors Center. Free. (410) 974-3400.

Governor's Mansion. State Circle and School Street. Built in the late 1860s and remodeled in Georgian style in 1936, this charming, three-story brick residence has been the official dwelling of Maryland's governors since 1870. The gardens and the interior were extensively renovated during the reign of Governor William Donald Schaefer in the late 1980s. An open house is offered to visitors each year during the Christmas season. Tours at any other time must be arranged individually. Free. (410) 974-3531.

St. Anne's Church. Church Circle. Just a short block from State Circle is St. Anne's, situated centrally in Church Circle. It is the third building to be erected on the foundation of what was Maryland's first brick church. Begun in 1700, the first church stood until just before the Revolution, when it was torn down. Remaining from this earlier edifice is the communion silver bearing the coat-of-arms of its donor, William III, who presented the gift to the parish in 1695. Sir

Robert Eden, the last colonial governor of Maryland, is buried in the church graveyard. Free. Open continuously. (410) 267-9333.

Chase-Lloyd House. The corner of King George Street and Maryland Avenue. This tall, imposing residence is one of the most elegant reminders of Annapolis' colonial era. It was begun in 1769 by Judge Samuel Chase, a signer of the Declaration of Independence. Unfortunately, Judge Chase was unable to financially support its completion. In 1771 it was acquired by Colonel Edward Lloyd IV, a wealthy tobacco grower. Later, Colonel Lloyd V became governor of Maryland and embellished the residence with marble mantels from Italy, decorated ceilings, ornate carvings, and wrought silver door latches and hinges. Fee. (410) 263-2723.

Hammond-Harwood House. Located at 19 Maryland Avenue. Purported to be one of the most perfect examples of fine Georgian architecture in America, this residence was designed and ornamented in 1774 by William Buckland, master craftsman. The exterior is salmon-colored brick with simple lines. The house, furnished in the style of the period, is noted for its beautiful woodwork such as the exquisitely carved shutters in the dining room. The entranceway and door are considered to be one of the most beautiful (and often photographed) in America. Traditional decorations add a special touch to Christmas season tours. Fee. (410) 269-1714.

St. John's College. College Avenue. Stroll under towering trees and around the cool, green lawns of one of America's oldest campuses. Chartered in 1784, its well-known alumni include Francis Scott Key. Standing at the center of the campus is **McDowell Hall,** which was begun in 1742 as the intended residence of Governor Thomas Bladen. Excessive costs caused the Lower House to vote against further building, and its completion was not until 1784 when the land and the house were given to St. John's College. Today it is used as the Administrative Building.

As you stand in front of McDowell Hall, you will see the famous **Liberty Tree.** This giant tulip poplar has endured through more than 400 years of history. Also located here is the **Dr. Charles Carroll-The Barrister-House** (c. 1724), which was moved to the campus in 1957 from Main Street. Free. (410) 263-2371.

William Paca House and Garden. Located at 186 Prince George Street. Built in 1763, this lovely Georgian residence was the winter home of William Paca, signer of the Declaration of Independence and governor of Maryland. The gardens are an outstanding part of this historic site. The two-acre terraced garden is a restoration of the original and features a Chinese trellis bridge, domed pavilion, and a fish-shaped pond. Tours of both house and garden are available. Fee. (410) 263-5553.

The Charles Carroll House of Annapolis. Located at 107 Duke of Gloucester Street (behind St. Mary's Church). Recently restored and opened to the public, this was the home of the wealthiest man in the colonies and the only Catholic to sign the Declaration of Independence. The three-acre estate, built during the 1770s, overlooks Spa Creek and was Carroll's primary dwelling until 1821. Fee. (410) 269-1737.

Return via State Circle to US-50 west to I-97, and follow reverse routing to Baltimore.

WHERE TO EAT

The Maryland Inn. Church Circle and Main Street. The inn was built on a piece of ground originally set aside for the use of the town drummer in 1694. In the 1770s, an elegant brick house was adjoined to the inn by Thomas Hyde, an Annapolis merchant. Today it continues to play host to guests and diners in its charming colonial rooms. The King of France Tavern, Treaty of Paris Dining Room, and the King's Wine Cellar offer day trip visitors hospitality, Maryland style. Traditional Maryland fare. $$; ☐. (410) 263-2641. Convenient maps of historic Annapolis are available at the Inn.

Chick and Ruth's Delly. Located at 165 Main Street. In this unpretentious, popular gathering spot you'll hear conversations ranging from pastrami to politics. Great sandwiches include an assortment of twenty-six specialties named for various state and local politicians. $; No ☐. (410) 269-6737.

CHESTERTOWN, MD

This charming little town is situated on the banks of the peaceful Chester River and exemplifies the easy, country living of Maryland's Eastern Shore. It is renowned for its waterfront homes, built during the Revolutionary period, which can be seen from the Chester River Bridge. Georgian mansions along the water remind us of the town's history, rooted in the Revolutionary era of the 1700s. Chestertown is an excellent place for a walking tour. Examples of period architecture and brickwork abound, much of it in private homes. Downtown Chestertown offers a variety of shops. From Baltimore take M–2 south to US–50/301 east across the Chesapeake Bay Bridge. Continue on US–301 to M–213 north to Chestertown.

WHERE TO GO

Geddes-Piper House. Church Alley. This example of an eighteenth-century Philadelphia town house is open to the public. It is a handsome, three-story brick house built between 1730 and 1754. Currently occupied by the Kent County Historical Society, it houses a collection of old maps and eighteenth-century furniture. Free. (410) 778-3499.

Walking Tours. Chestertown. Additional information on the historic houses and walking tours can be obtained from the Historical Society and from the Kent County Chamber of Commerce, (410) 778-0416.

51

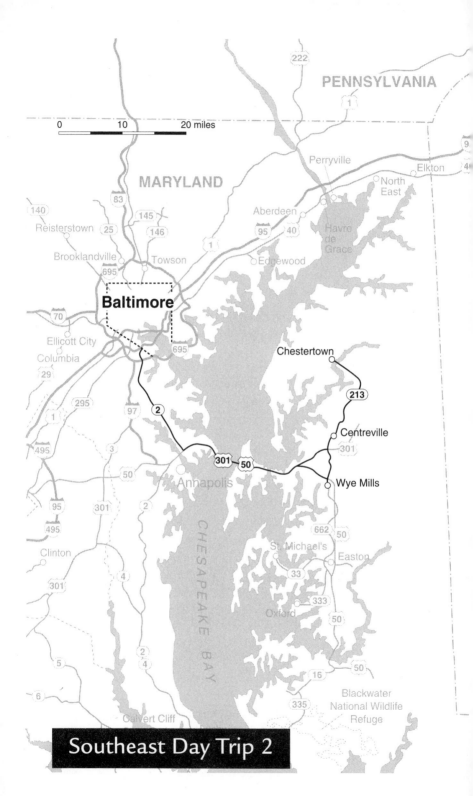

Southeast Day Trip 2

CENTREVILLE, MD

Centreville was established around the **Queen Anne's County Courthouse,** one of the two eighteenth-century courthouses in existence in Maryland today. The courthouse has remained in use continuously since 1792. Located at 120 North Commerce Street, the building of white-painted brick contrasts with the greens of the boxwood hedge and the tree-shaded square. The masonry is laid in the Flemish bond design. A large **statue of Queen Anne,** by Elizabeth Gordon Chandler, stands on the courthouse green. From Chestertown, take M–213 south to Centreville.

WHERE TO GO

Wright's Chance. Located at 119 South Commerce Street. This 1740 plantation house was relocated to Centreville within walking distance from the courthouse. It features the original wood paneling and glass windowpanes. It now houses a museum and the headquarters for the county historical society. It is furnished in the style of the period. Fee. (410) 758–3010.

Tucker House. Located at 124 South Commerce Street. This is the working museum for the Queen Anne's County Historical Society. Guided tours are available. Fee. For information regarding the properties of the historical society, call (410) 758–3010.

WYE MILLS, MD

Continue your driving day trip to the town that is centered around the Old Wye Mill. These peaceful flatlands of the Eastern Shore provided the setting for the plantation homes of famous Maryland history-makers such as the Paca and Tilghman families. **Wye Hall,** located on nearby Wye Island, was destroyed in 1879 by fire. It was the mansion home of William Paca. **Wye Plantation,** originally owned by the Tilghman family, is a seventeenth-century structure that time has spared. Located on Wye Neck Road, the estate is now privately owned and raises purebred Angus cattle. From Centreville, take M–213 south to US–50. Drive south to the junction of M–404 and Wye Mills.

WHERE TO GO

Old Wye Grist Mill. At the junction of US–50 south and M–404, turn right and drive west for about ¼ mile to the mill. This site has maintained a mill since colonial days. Flour for the troops of George Washington was ground here and, under private ownership, it continued to function for an estimated 250 years. Be sure to stop here and walk around the mill. The mill is usually open and grinding meal for purchase on weekends (11:00 A.M. to 4:00 P.M.) from April through December. (410) 827-6909.

Wye Oak. Continue west on M–404 to M–662 south. Near this junction, situated on twenty-nine acres, is the country's only one-tree state forest. The tree stands close to the entrance of the park off M–662 and is well marked. The Wye Oak is Maryland's state tree, measures 50 feet in circumference, 95 feet in height, and is approximately 400 years old. Any fallen limbs are artistically carved into prestigious gavels, and seedlings from the tree are sold by the State Forest Service. Open year-round. Free.

Old Wye Church. Located within walking distance of the Wye Oak on M–662 is one of the oldest Episcopal churches in America. The interior of this church, built in 1721, features high box pews, a hanging pulpit, a gallery bearing the Royal Arms of England, and original communion pieces dating from 1737. Nearby is the reconstructed vestry house, which was erected on the original foundations and furnished in eighteenth-century antiques. Also located here is the parish house, built in 1957 in eighteenth-century style. Open mid-April through November. Services are held each Sunday at 11:00 A.M. Free; donations accepted. (410) 827-8484.

SOUTHEAST DAY TRIP 3

Easton, MD
Oxford, MD
St. Michaels, MD

Worth More Time:
Blackwater National Wildlife Refuge, MD

EASTON, MD

The "Colonial Capital of the Eastern Shore" earned its title due to the centralization of administrative offices here for all Eastern Shore counties. Dating back to the 1700s, Easton was established around the Talbot County Courthouse. During colonial times, the village developed slowly. The **Old Third Haven Quaker Meeting House** is the only building from that era. Lord Baltimore attended services here and William Penn preached on its front lawn. After the Revolution, however, Easton grew rapidly. Much of the reason for its expansion is its central location in relationship to neighboring counties. Easton claims the first newspaper on the Eastern Shore (1790), the first bank (1805), and the first steamboat line to Baltimore (1817).

The street plan of Easton dates back to 1785. Local streets were named by Jeremiah Banning, a Talbot County landowner. Washington Street is the principal business corridor.

Continue along Washington Street to well-maintained brick buildings, which still display some original external woodwork.

The buildings on the central square were restored to a Federal-period style in the 1950s, and subsequent construction in the area has kept this theme. The town is charming and lends itself well to walking and biking tours. Clothing shops display the casual look; those with a penchant for geese and mallards will find much to their taste.

Easton is host to an annual fall **Waterfowl Festival,** which showcases expert decoy carving and painting by local artists. Fall

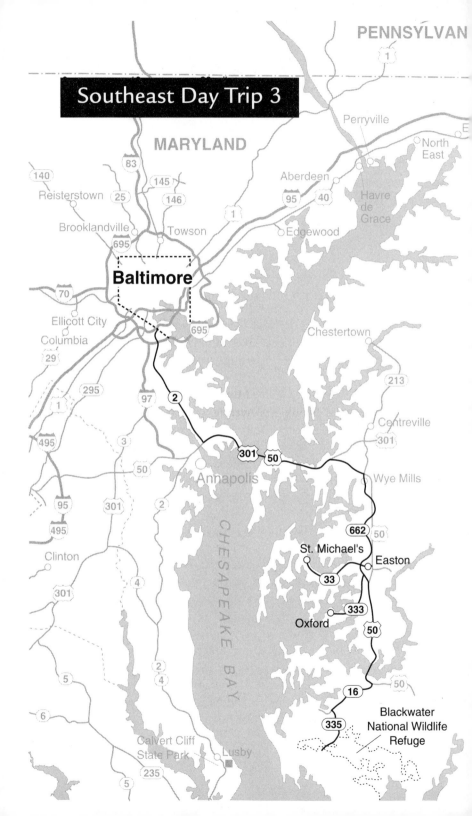

fills the area hotels with avid sportsmen seeking their share of ducks. Window displays in realtors' offices tempt visitors to retire to waterfront acreage. Pubs and restaurants offer congeniality and well-prepared seafood.

From Baltimore take M-2 south to US-50/301 east, and cross the Chesapeake Bay Bridge. Follow US-50 south to M-331 west to Easton. Or, if you are coming from Wye Mills (Day Trip 2, this sector), simply follow the same route south on US-50.

WHERE TO GO

The Historical Society of Talbot County. Located at 25 South Washington Street. The Society is located in the **Stevens House,** a restored building built by a Quaker cabinetmaker in 1810. The Federal town house is now a museum featuring period furnishings, a garden, and rotating exhibits. Fee. (410) 822-0773.

The Third Haven Quaker Meeting House. South on Washington Street past Brookletts Avenue, several blocks south of the historical society. This house is believed to be the oldest frame building dedicated to religious meetings in America. William Penn preached here, and Lord Baltimore attended services here. Erected in 1682, the clapboard structure still contains the original broad plank floors and straight-backed benches. While not routinely open for tours, it is definitely worth walking around for a view of one of our country's earliest shrines to religious freedom. Free. (410) 822-0293.

The Academy of the Arts. Harrison and South Streets. Here you can see a variety of works by local artists. (410) 822-0455.

Guided Tours of Easton. Arrangements for special guided tours (fee) of the area can be made by calling (410) 822-0773.

WHERE TO EAT

The Tidewater Inn. Dover and Harrison Streets. Traditional decor with a fine Maryland kitchen. Consistently well-prepared food is served here with Eastern Shore hospitality. If you choose this as an overnight resting spot, reservations are recommended. Lunch, $$; dinner, $$$; ☐. (410) 822-1300.

OXFORD, MD

Early records document Oxford's existence in 1668. Situated on the Tred Avon River, the town flourished in export trading and was rivaled only by the port of Annapolis. Oxford was overshadowed by the bustling growth of Baltimore and slipped into a decline. After the Civil War, however, shipbuilding, oystering, and fish-packing revived the town's economy, which has remained stable ever since.

Despite its early beginning, Oxford's architecture has more nineteenth-century design than eighteenth-century. The city has remained relatively untouched by tasteless commercialism and signs. Peaceful, well-maintained homes sit like gems on green velvet cushions. Stroll through side streets and coves to small docks berthing privately owned sailcraft. Grab a taste of the Chesapeake Bay from one of the several casual and carryout seafood kitchens located here. And see The Strand, an impressive block of homes of variable architecture propitiously placed along the Tred Avon River. A small but delightful beach lines the bank of the Tred Avon. Local residents bring their picnic hampers and spread blankets for a summer retreat here.

The shops in Oxford are not as sophisticated as in Easton; they offer interesting bargains in a country store setting. The public park offers a pleasing access to the quiet beauty of the Tred Avon River.

In Easton, drive south on Washington Street to Peach Blossom Road (M–333). Drive south on M–333 directly into Oxford.

WHERE TO GO

The Oxford Cemetery. Located on M–333 just outside the town of Oxford is the historic Oxford Cemetery. Headstones and gravemarkers quietly understate the magnitude of the contributions to Maryland history made by those buried here. Among the most famous buried here are Colonel Tench Tilghman (1744–1786) and his wife, Anna Maria. Colonel Tilghman became a wealthy merchant before the outbreak of the Revolutionary War. His support of the independence movement caused great family strain, for his father was a loyalist. Tilghman served General Washington as his secretary and then as his aide-de-camp. When the victory at Yorktown was secured, it was Tilghman who carried the news of Cornwallis's surrender to Congress in Philadelphia. Descendants erected the **Tench Tilghman Monument** here in commemoration.

The Morris House. Morris Street and The Strand. Built about 1701, this structure is part of the charming **Robert Morris Inn.** Architecturally, it is a tribute to the style of the eighteenth century. In 1703, an English trading company bought the house as a residence for Robert Morris, a representative of the Oxford firm's shipping interests. Robert, Jr., his son, came from England in 1747 to join him and went on to be a signer of the Declaration of Independence and a noted financier of the Continental Army. Original floorings, mural wall coverings, and careful restoration add to the flavor of this favorite inn and dining spot. (410) 226-5111.

The Academy (Bratt House). Several doors up from The Strand on Morris Street is the distinctive gray clapboard building that served as part of the Maryland Military School, established in 1848. A box garden now exists where the main house stood before it was destroyed by fire in 1855. The remaining landmark has a pilastered facade and cupola atop a low hipped roof. The box hedge and the wrought-iron front porch also remain. Not open to the public.

The Oxford-Bellevue Ferry. M-333 at the Tred Avon River. Also known as the **Tred Avon Ferry,** it is believed to be the oldest free-running (not attached to a cable) ferry in the country. Initiated in 1683, it was oar-propelled until 1886 when power service began. Take a break from the road, place your car on the ferry, and connect to Bellevue on your way to St. Michaels. (410) 745-9023.

WHERE TO EAT

The Robert Morris Inn. Morris Street and The Strand. This elegant high spot of the Eastern Shore is dedicated to a tradition of quality, with consistently good food and excellent service. The inn is featured in such publications as *Classic Country Inns of America* and *America's Historic Inns and Taverns.* Magazines such as *Southern Living, Good Housekeeping, Town and County,* and *Better Homes and Gardens* have recommended it in their reviews. James Michener enjoyed the broiled crab cakes here while he lived in the area during the writing of *Chesapeake.* Reservations are not accepted, as guests are served on a first-come, first-served basis. Both the inn and the restaurant have a quiet, conservative atmosphere. The proprietors do not welcome children under age ten or large groups. With that in mind, if it still meets your criteria, do plan to stay the night here. Excellence prevails in the guest rooms also, where tasteful period furnishings give you a sense of visiting the past. Accommodations range from the modestly priced singles with shared baths, to the more substantially priced combinations of bedroom and sitting room.

The inn is open daily for dining and lodging, except Christmas holidays. In the tap room, casual dress is acceptable. In the dining room, coats are required for men, except from Memorial Day through Labor Day. Lunch, $$; dinner, $$$; ☐. (410) 226-5111.

ST. MICHAELS, MD

The unspoiled heritage of St. Michaels is reminiscent of the same economic growth, decline, and restabilization experienced by its neighbor, Oxford. Accessible by water on two sides and once heavily timbered, St. Michaels became a center for shipbuilding and prosperity. The industry rose to prominence during the Revolutionary War but declined around 1830 as a result of diminishing timber and the rise of Baltimore as a major competitor. The industry was somewhat revived in the following decade, and the seafood and agricultural processing businesses now sustain this modest town. A yachting haven, St. Michaels hosts a very popular sailing regatta each August on the Miles River west of town.

Biking is especially good in St. Michaels, as in Oxford and Easton, due to the quiet, level streets. Biking also affords a sense of closer contact with the roadside sights and quaint shops. Some of the antiques shops here are for the more serious collector, but many are a fascinating hodgepodge of memorabilia and Americana. These colorful caches are definitely worth a visit. Depart on the Tred Avon Ferry and pick up M-329 west to M-33 west directly into St. Michaels.

WHERE TO GO

St. Mary's Square Museum. "The Green," located between Talbot and Mulberry Streets. This museum, constructed in the seventeenth century of axe-hewn half timbers and filled with local memorabilia, is located on a plot of ground around which St. Michaels was built. Fee. (410) 745-9561.

Chesapeake Bay Maritime Museum. In St. Michaels, turn right at Mill Street. The Maritime Museum is located on a peninsula in the harbor of St. Michaels. It features the Hooper Straight Lighthouse, indigenous sailing craft, maritime exhibits, a boat-building workshop, and a special display of carved waterfowl. (Fee). Maps for self-guided walking tours of St. Michaels can also be obtained here. (410) 745-2916. Return via US-50 north and follow reverse routing to Baltimore.

WHERE TO EAT

Inn at Perry Cabin. Located at 308 Watkins Lane. This fine restaurant and elegant inn with a variety of rooms and suites is owned by Sir Bernard Ashley, widower of Laura Ashley, and decorated in her style and design. The restaurant offers wonderful English-Continental cuisine. $$$$; □. (410) 745-2200 or (800) 722-2949.

WORTH MORE TIME

BLACKWATER NATIONAL WILDLIFE REFUGE, MD

Each year, thousands of migrating birds fly south to the warmer marshlands of Maryland's Eastern Shore. Wintering Canada geese flock to this refuge during November and December. Tourists can observe this natural phenomenon from driving paths that link the fields and streams. Bring your camera to capture the other wildlife in this refuge as well. If you choose, you may bicycle through the refuge. Climb the ranger's tower to view the flocks of birds and listen to their soulful honking. This destination is slightly beyond the two-hour limitations. Plan to see it, if you have the time, or if you plan to stay overnight on the Eastern Shore. A visitor's center in the refuge provides interpretive material and maps of trails and roads. Fee. (410) 228-2677.

From St. Michaels take US-50 south to M-16 southwest. Then take M-335 south along the well-signed route to Key Wallace Drive.

WHERE TO GO

Old Trinity Church. M-16 at Church Street. While en route to Blackwater Wildlife Refuge, you'll pass the oldest church in the country that is still in use. The church was established in 1675, and the adjoining graveyard is the resting place for many famous Marylanders. (410) 228-2940.

Wild Goose Brewery. Located at 20 Washington Street, Cambridge. This is the Eastern Shore's only microbrewery at this writing. Take a tour, then sample the ale, amber, or lager. Free. (410) 221-1121.

Tilghman Island. M-33 at the Chesapeake Bay. This island is home port for a large part of the bay's skipjack fleet. Visit Tilghman and Fairbank, the two small fishing villages on this island that feature many oyster-shucking and crab-packing plants. Enjoy the bay's savory delights at one of the seafood restaurants on the island. (410) 822-4606.

WHERE TO EAT

Harrison's Country Inn. Route 33, Tilghman's Island. This is home base for Captain "Buddy" Harrison and his forebears who began bringing in guests from Baltimore during the long hot summers in the city. An inn, restaurant, and gathering point for fishing and hunting trips, it has become a traditional spot for folks who enjoy well-prepared, fresh, but not fancy seafood overlooking the water. $-$$; ☐. (410) 886-2123.

Day Trips from Baltimore

Our next day trip destination is in southern Maryland, where extensive plantations were a testimony to social and economic achievements. Large landowners thrived on the increasing demand for tobacco—both locally and in exports. Livestock and nontobacco crops such as corn and wheat were also grown in these self-sustaining communities. Overwhelmingly rural, southern Maryland did not play an active part in the Revolutionary War. The area's agricultural lifestyle was largely untouched by the volatile times. Fertile soil and navigable waterways lent themselves well to tobacco production. As independent landowners prospered, their wealth was frequently applied to the acquisition and clearing of new land for farming.

A drive through southern Maryland is a drive through three centuries of Maryland history. The National Colonial Farm Museum pays tribute to the agricultural heritage that still predominates in the region. Roadside farmers' markets attest to that, offering a tempting array of fresh produce, home-baked items, preserves, jellies, and local crafts.

In Prince George's County, recorded history began in 1608 with a visit from Captain John Smith. Active efforts here have preserved much of its heritage for the visitor of today, and it is said that you'll see more eighteenth-century architecture in this area than in all of Williamsburg, Virginia.

Modern high-tech industries have also found a home in southern Maryland. Pioneering companies embark on research and development in solar cell production, microelectronics, and biomedical research.

Agriculture, history, and high tech are all found in the surprising southern reaches of Maryland.

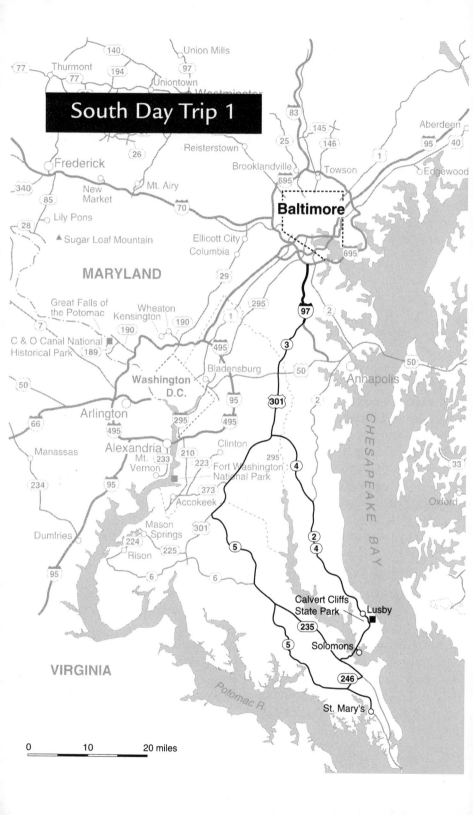

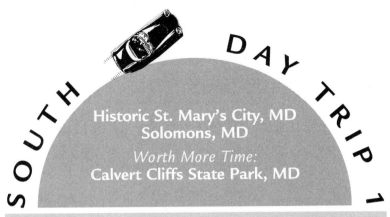

SOUTH

DAY TRIP 1

Historic St. Mary's City, MD
Solomons, MD
Worth More Time:
Calvert Cliffs State Park, MD

HISTORIC ST. MARY'S CITY, MD

The countryside of southern Maryland has changed little since the mid-1600s when the first English colonists settled seeking religious freedom, new lives, and adventure in the New World. Even today, there are many significant churches dating back to the early 1700s. Although this trip presses the limits of our day trip definition, it is certainly worth the effort to get an early morning start as there are numerous sites in southern Maryland that are worth more time.

Soon after the founding of St. Mary's City, Maryland's first capital, tobacco became the dominant crop, giving the area a strong southern culture that still prevails. Maryland tobacco is especially prized in Europe, even today, as some of the world's finest. As you drive through the region in summertime, you'll see fields filled with the bright green tobacco plants. In early fall, slatted barns are filled with curing crops waiting for next year's auction.

Meticulous re-creation of the original St. Mary's City settlement has been under way for more than three decades in St. Mary's City. The town lands were granted in 1636 by Lord Baltimore on special terms for early settlers. The original settlement consisted of approximately 1,200 acres. Today, about 800 acres comprise Historic St. Mary's City.

In 1640, at least ten dwellings, a forge, a mill, and a Catholic chapel were scattered across thirteen separate tracts. The seventeenth-century capital was located here although no traditional clustered development began before the 1660s. In 1678, there were as many as eighteen structures in St. Mary's City, including the State

House, the secretary's office, and a prison. Most of the others were lodgings, inns, and offices for lawyers and clerks, all involved with the operation of the government. The State House was constructed in 1676, but masonry skills lacked, and by 1693, the walls were reported to "leane out on each side of the Staire case." This was at least part of the reason to construct a centrally located statehouse. By 1708, there were no voters to hold an election and St. Mary's City lost its representation in the legislature. By 1720, the town disappeared completely. In the early 1990s, three lead coffins were unearthed, causing a great deal of speculation about the remains they contained. Several scientific and federal agencies were called in to perform various tests to determine if the bodies were those of early Maryland aristocrats. Find out about the results, when you visit St. Mary's City.

Today, however, the heritage of the settlement comes to life with accurately reconstructed seventeenth-century buildings, a working tobacco plantation, a world-class archeological dig, living history and drama, historic areas, hiking and nature areas, excellent displays, a gift shop, and a wonderful restaurant.

A visit to authentically restored Historic St. Mary's City makes you realize that the depiction of early colonial times usually created in Disney films and TV programs is glamorous compared to the real life version. It's a learning experience for all ages.

Historic St. Mary's City is open to the public from late March to the end of November, Wednesday through Sunday. The main entrance is on Rosecroft Road. Fee. (800) SMC-1634 or (301) 862-0990.

From Baltimore City, take M-3, US-301 south; turn left to M-5 Waldorf-Leonardtown Road. Continue directly to Historic St. Mary's City.

WHERE TO GO

Visitors Center. Begin at the restored early-twentieth-century farm buildings that house the information, ticket, and orientation areas, and auditorium, archeological displays, and historical exhibits. The gift shop is also located here. (301) 862-0990.

Godiah Spray Tobacco Plantation. This is a complete working reconstruction of a seventeenth-century tobacco farm including a rustic dwelling, kitchen garden, animals, crops, barns, and living history presentations, during summer months. (301) 862-0990.

Maryland *Dove*. Docked on the St. Mary's River, this replica of Lord Baltimore's square-rigged pinnace, which transported supplies for the original settlers, is available for boarding and close inspection. You'll enjoy chatting with the crew members. The original *Dove* accompanied the *Ark* on the first voyage to Maryland in 1634. (301) 862-0990.

State House of 1676. This is a replica of Maryland's first public building. Inside you'll see historical exhibits and enjoy living history presentations. (301) 862-0990.

Old Trinity Episcopal Church. This was built shortly after 1829 with bricks salvaged from the State House of 1676. The grounds contain historical markers commemorating the history of Maryland. (410) 862-4597.

WHERE TO EAT

Farthing's Ordinary. Make this a "must" stop in your visit. Pause and refresh in this victualling house and inn serving wonderful colonial foods and beverages, inside or under the grape arbor. Reasonably priced food served by friendly and efficient costumed personnel. $$; ☐. (301) 862-0988.

Penwick House. Route 4 at Ferry Landing Road, Dunkirk, MD. Delightful food in a wonderful atmosphere. Owner Audrey Davenport has done a wonderful job in creating the charm of southern Maryland and re-creating some of the most famous regional dishes. A great spot for a Sunday brunch. After lunch or dinner, browse in the gift shop. $$; ☐. (410) 257-7077.

SOLOMONS, MD

After the Civil War, Isaac Solomon established an oyster cannery on this island. Eastern Shore people worked with him, fishing and canning. Situated at the mouth of the Patuxent River and Chesapeake Bay, this was an ideal location. On the mainland side of the island is a landlocked harbor serving as an anchorage for the fishing fleet and the many boats stopping here on the Inland Waterway. On the Patuxent side of the island is one of the East Coast's great natural harbors, 2 miles wide and often more than 100 feet deep. Although its location is ideal in respect to water, it also had disadvantages. Solomons was too far from railroads and cities, and too close to Baltimore and Norfolk to be commercially successful. Solomons is coming into its own today with tourism. From St. Mary's City, take M-5 north to right on M-246 (Great Mills Road) to M-235 north to Lexington Park. Here, you may want to visit the Naval Air Museum at the Patuxent Naval Air Test Station. M-235 to M-4 north; cross the Governor Thomas Johnson Memorial Bridge to Solomons.

WHERE TO GO

Calvert Marine Museum and Lighthouse. Virtually at the end of the Johnson Memorial Bridge you'll find the Solomons Visitors Center and across the street, the Calvert Marine Museum. In this unusual museum, you'll find boats, models, carvings, fossils, working areas, and wonderful displays depicting life and work in the Chesapeake Bay region. Here, you can board the *Wm. B. Tennison,* built in 1899, for a cruise around Solomons. Be sure to visit the restored Drum Point Lighthouse and the J. C. Lore Oyster House, which features a boat-building exhibit and local seafood industry artifacts. Fee. (410) 326-2042.

Solomons Island. When you leave the museum, park your vehicle in the public parking area and take a walking tour of Solomons Island. There are numerous restaurants, antiques and gift shops, inns, pubs, and charter and boat rental facilities along the way. Return to Baltimore by heading north on M-2/4 to north US-3/301.

WHERE TO EAT

The Dry Dock. Zahnisher's Marina, C Street, Solomons Island. An innovative menu featuring seasonal local favorites. Intimate atmosphere overlooking Back Creek and Solomons Harbor. $$; ☐. (410) 326-4817.

Lighthouse Inn Restaurant. M-2. Solomons Island. Featuring traditional seafood dishes, you can belly up to the outdoor raw bar, or dine indoors by candlelight, both with great views of the water. In summer months, enjoy lunch and frozen cocktails on the deck overlooking the harbor. $$; ☐. (410) 326-2445.

WORTH MORE TIME

CALVERT CLIFFS STATE PARK, MD

Hike through the 1,600-acre state park to the fantastic Cliffs of Calvert. Some 30 miles of fossil-embedded cliffs tower high above the Chesapeake Bay. More than 600 varieties of Miocene fossils, fifteen to twenty million years old, are found along the beach. (410) 888-1410. M-2/4 to Lusby, north of Solomons Island.

Calvert Cliffs Nuclear Power Plant and Visitors Center. M-2/4 north of Solomons Island. Here, in a nineteenth-century tobacco barn, there's an information center with agricultural and archeological exhibits and a hands-on energy and nuclear power display. From the visitors' overlook, one can see across Chesapeake Bay and view Maryland's first nuclear power plant. Free. (301) 872-5389.

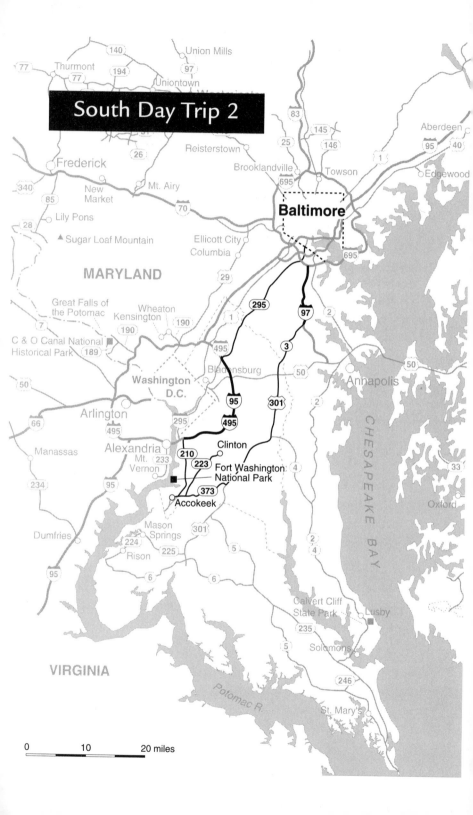

South Day Trip 2

ACCOKEEK, MD

According to early documentation by Captain John Smith, Accokeek is situated on the site of Moyanone, a Piscataway Indian village. While the village was burned in 1622, numerous artifacts have been unearthed here with the cooperation of the Smithsonian Institution. Archeological and anthropological quests have yielded thousands of skeletons, indicating that the site was occupied for several hundred years. A museum located in the public library displays some of these finds. From Baltimore, take US-3 south to US-301 south. Take M-373 west, just past the M-210 junction of Accokeek.

WHERE TO GO

National Colonial Farm Museum. Located at 3400 Bryant Point Road at the Potomac River, about 3 miles west of the M-373 and M-210 junction. Operated by the Accokeek Foundation, the museum is an example of a functioning eighteenth-century Tidewater farm. Located on the Potomac River, it is in the central portion of Piscataway Park and commands a view of Mount Vernon, the home of the first president of the United States. It is an appropriate setting for the exhibition and demonstration of the agricultural methods, crops, livestock, and everyday living of colonial days.

Visitor information and tour arrangements can be obtained at the gatehouse. Included on the tour are the colonial crop demonstrations; an herb garden that produces more than fifty varieties used for medicinal, cosmetic, and culinary purposes; a delightful orchard, pond, and chestnut grove; and a variety of livestock typical of the times. The foundation has done a very faithful job in presenting the modern-day visitor with a window to the world on the colonial era. Fee. (301) 283–2115.

CLINTON, MD

Clinton's lure is almost entirely attributable to John and Mary Surratt. The town became known as Surrattsville when John was appointed postmaster in 1854. The family house and tavern served as a local post office, a resting place for travelers, a public dining room, and a local polling place. It was also a "safe" house for Confederate couriers.

American history enthusiasts and Abraham Lincoln buffs will remember it for the deeds of Mary Surratt. In 1865, Lincoln's assassin, John Wilkes Booth, and David E. Herold stopped here on the way to the home of Dr. Samuel Mudd. For her part in taking in these travelers, Mrs. Surratt was charged, found guilty, and hanged for alleged complicity in the plot to assassinate Lincoln. She was the first woman to be executed by the federal government. Controversy still prevails over her innocence, as much of the damaging testimony was unsubstantiated or extracted from unreliable sources. From Accokeek, take M–373 east to M–223 north to Clinton.

WHERE TO GO

Historic Surratt House. Located at 9110 Brandywine Road. The family house, tavern, and post office were built in 1852 by John Surratt. In 1965, it was donated to the National Capital Park and Planning Commission. The property is recognized as having historic significance, and restoration was begun with the assistance of local citizens. Today visitors may tour the site (closed January and February) assisted by costumed guides and hear the intriguing details of the saga of Mary Surratt. Fee. (301) 868–1121.

FORT WASHINGTON NATIONAL PARK, MD

Fort Washington is an imposing example of the first fortifications erected for the defense of the nation's capital. George Washington selected this ideal elevated terrain along the Potomac River in 1795. While the fort erected here in 1808 commanded an excellent view of the river for miles, it was inadequate in construction and poorly planned. The British destroyed this earlier fort during the War of 1812. Major Charles L'Enfant, planner and designer of Washington, DC, immediately set about constructing the present fort. A quarrel with the War Department interrupted his work, and Lieutenant Colonel Warren K. Armistad completed the construction in 1824. A visit to Fort Washington National Park is an excellent opportunity to see an example of early-nineteenth-century strategy in defense and garrison life.

To get here from Clinton, take M–223 southwest to where it becomes Farmington Road (just west of Piscataway). From Farmington Road, turn right on M–210 and drive north to Old Fort Road and turn left. Drive west to Fort Washington Road and turn left. Drive west to Fort Washington Park.

WHERE TO GO

Fort Washington. M–210, Silesia. One of the most interesting old military structures in the country, Fort Washington has been altered little since its construction in 1824. It is an enclosed masonry fortification entered by a drawbridge across the dry moat at the sally port. From above the main gateway you can see the entire 833-foot outline of the fort. Approximately 60 feet below the main fort is the outer V-shaped water battery, begun by Major Charles L'Enfant, as well as the ditch on the southwest face and most of the ditch on the northeast face. They are still in an excellent state of preservation. A double stairway connects the parade ground with a tunnel leading to the lower construction.

Two half-bastions overlook and command the river above and below the fort. Below the ramparts of these two structures are the gun positions. From these levels (water battery, casement positions, and ramparts), guns could deliver a devastating fire against an enemy fleet on the Potomac.

The front of the structure, built of solid stone and brick masonry, is about 7 feet thick. On the parade ground are the officers' quarters and the soldiers' barracks. Flanking each of these structures is a magazine. A guardroom, containing two narrow cells, and the office of the commanding officer are in the main gateway structure. Civil War weapons and garrison life demonstrations are regularly scheduled. Fee. For details, call (301) 763-4600.

From Fort Washington, the most time-efficient approach to Baltimore begins with re-routing on Fort Washington Road east to M-210 north. Pick up I-95 south around the southeast perimeter of Washington to exit 22 and the Baltimore-Washington Parkway (M-295 northeast) into Baltimore.

WORTH MORE TIME

Dr. Samuel A. Mudd Museum. Dr. Samuel Mudd Road, Waldorf, MD. Dr. Mudd was the physician who set the broken leg of Lincoln assassin, John Wilkes Booth. He was later imprisoned and falsely implicated in the plot. The museum features various exhibits and the original furnishings. Call for schedule. Fee. (301) 934-8464.

Day Trips from Baltimore

Travel southwest to a blend of past, present, and future—the old and historic coupled with the community of today and tomorrow. From Beltway to backroads we'll take a day trip through two of America's earliest states—Maryland and Virginia—and to our nation's capital.

Rural peace and small town quiet prevailed in this area throughout the nineteenth century. Today, one-third of Montgomery County, Maryland, is residential or commercial; one-third is preserved for agricultural land; and the remaining is dedicated to open space, including more than 26,000 acres of parkland. This area is unique in its beauty and its location. Easy access is afforded by major interstate highways and the Capital Beltway.

The residents of Howard County, Maryland, were advised in 1963 of the advent of Columbia, a new city planned to avoid the sprawl and inconveniences common to many burgeoning cities. Today, Columbia continues to develop toward the needs of the family of tomorrow.

To the southwest are cities of the past, which trace their history to the pre–Revolutionary War period. These historic districts offer preserved Victorian architecture, brick sidewalks, and tree-shaded streets that keep the city's old flavor alive.

Virginia's northern region is the gateway to a state that boasts four centuries of American development and achievement. The state's visitors are treated to majestic mountains, underground caves, and vibrant cities offering a variety of shopping possibilities.

Rich in historic treasures, northern Virginia's attractions include Old Town Alexandria, numerous Civil War battlefields, and Mount Vernon, home of George Washington.

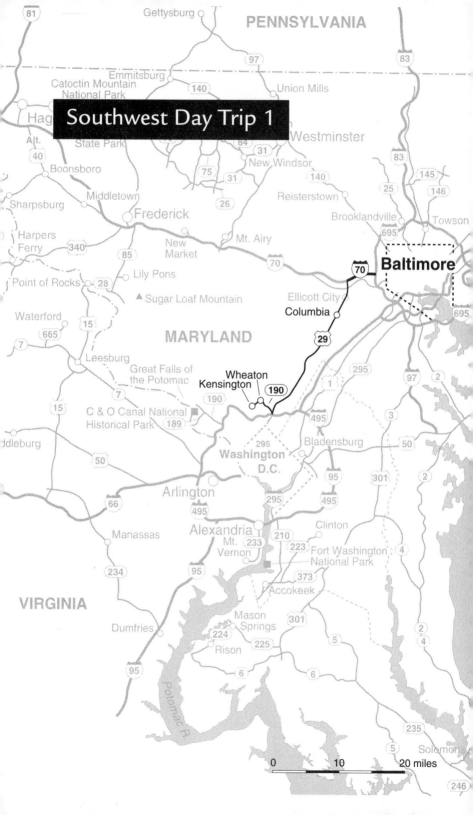

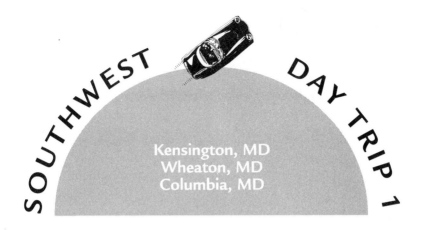

KENSINGTON, MD

Kensington begins a day trip of fascinating stops. You'll pass through Howard County and rub shoulders with Columbia, a town that offers shopping and browsing.

From Baltimore take I-95 southwest toward Washington. At M-175 drive west to Columbia. Then, pick up US-29 south, which offers time-efficient and scenic routing through Howard and Montgomery counties. From US-29 south take I-495 west to exit 33 toward Kensington.

WHERE TO GO

Mormon Temple. Located at 9900 Stoneybrook Drive, Kensington. From exit 33A off I-495 west take Connecticut Avenue north. At the second traffic light, turn right onto Beach Drive. Follow Beach Drive to Stoneybrook Drive and turn left. This leads to the main entrance of the visitors center. Long before you arrive at Stoneybrook Drive, the Mormon Temple will loom before you like a fairyland castle. It is the largest structure dedicated to the Mormon Church east of the Mississippi. The temple has seven floors and is topped with six steeples. Atop one steeple is an angel weighing two and a half tons, with trumpet poised and gold-leafed robes. The $15 million building stands atop a gentle hill on fifty-seven acres overlooking the Capital Beltway. Standing sixteen stories tall and built on a solid rock foundation, the building is covered with nearly 175,000 square feet of white Alabama marble.

When the temple was completed in 1974, it was entirely open to the public for tours. Today, while the sanctuary of the temple is not available to the public, the visitors center offers tours of some rooms, movies, and a diorama of the history of the Mormon Church. The gardens that surround the facility offer excellent foregrounds for photos, especially those in proximity to the attractive little ponds. Open daily. Free. (301) 587-0144.

WHEATON, MD

Wheaton is a close, convenient neighbor to Kensington, so routing to your next destination is simple. From the Mormon Temple, return to Connecticut Avenue and pick up M–193 east toward Wheaton and the Wheaton Regional Park.

WHERE TO GO

Brookside Gardens. Located at 1500 Glenallan Avenue (between Randolph and Kemp Mill Roads), Wheaton Regional Park. The fifty-acre public garden is open year-round and features tropical plants, a stream, and a conservatory greenhouse. Special seasonal plantings, such as poinsettias during the Christmas holidays, are especially fine. The formal gardens are beautiful for walking and viewing. There are rose, azalea, and aquatic gardens. From early spring to the first frost, there is a wide variety of flowering plants. A special highlight is the Japanese-style garden and teahouse situated on an island with a reflecting pool. Brookside Gardens also offers lectures, courses, and workshops for the general public. Tours and special programs for adults and children are available. Free. (301) 949-8230.

National Capital Trolley Museum. Located at 1313 Bonifant Road, between Layhill and Notley Roads in Northwest Branch Regional Park. Streetcars or trolleys from Austria, Germany, and Washington, DC, are here to take you on a 1½-mile track in the park's countryside. Open weekends, the museum features lots of special events, mostly associated with the past . . . barbershop music, Dixieland concerts, and antique car shows. Fee. Call ahead for the schedule. (301) 384-6088.

COLUMBIA, MD

James Rouse is the dynamic developer of the "New Town" concept in America. Such instant successes as the shopping-dining formats of Faneuil Hall Market Place in Boston and Harborplace in Baltimore are but two of the tributes to his brand of genius. In 1981, more visitors strolled through Harborplace in Baltimore than Disney World in Orlando.

In the mid-1960s, Howard County residents saw Rouse sculpt an entirely new city out of 15,000 acres of rolling, green countryside. Columbia took shape within guidelines that ensured a harmonious interdependence of homes, businesses, churches, and commercial properties. An innovative community-based health care plan and local hospital deliver medical care with convenience and expediency. Subcommunities, or neighborhoods, are clustered around ample recreational facilities. Tasteful architecture and low-slung building complexes slip easily into the green, forested landscape.

Attractions include a shopping mall with more than one hundred opportunities to go for broke. Clothing, household items and furnishings, music stores, jewelers, and light fare dining spots are only a sample of the many shops and stops. The ubiquitous fountains and atria, which have been mimicked so frequently in other malls, add the peaceful sight and sound of flowing water complemented by rays of sunlight on lush plants.

In addition to the mall, there is a delightful Children's Zoo that is replete with farm animals. Nearby, the Merriweather Post Pavilion of Music is situated in a beautiful woodland setting and draws top-flight summertime entertainment ranging from the Washington National Symphony to pop performers. Enjoy reserved seats or picnic under the stars at the outer-margin grassy areas while you listen to the performances.

From Wheaton continue along M–193 east to US–29 north to Columbia. Or, if you plan to depart from Baltimore to make Columbia a single destination day trip, take US–40 west to US–29 south to Columbia. Return to Baltimore via US–29 north and US–40 east to the downtown area.

WHERE TO EAT

The Mall. Little Patuxent Parkway, Columbia. Strategically located amidst the one hundred or so shops in the mall are numerous eateries with varying fare. Make mental notes as you stroll along the corridors, then select your preference. Pizza, deli, and fried chicken places compete with those featuring unusual salads and croissant combinations. Take your pick. $; usually cash only.

King's Contrivance. Located at 10150 Shaker Drive at Route 32, Columbia. This has long been a favorite dining spot for a very special occasion and folks still drive for quite some way to enjoy lunch and dinner at this historic country estate. Food is mainly French with a tendency toward classic dishes. $$$; ☐. (410) 995-0500.

Early Mansions Tour:
Prince George's County, MD

PRINCE GEORGE'S COUNTY, MD

Maryland has often been described as America in miniature. Our nation's history has been carved in the state's shoreline, flatlands, and mountains. Prince George's County might well be called Maryland in miniature. Similarities between the development of the county and state, and the development of the country, reveal much about our political history. These similarities are seen through historical documents and surviving public buildings. The early mansion homes, however, provide a more personal view of life in Prince George's County and America.

In these residences, an elegant domestic and social lifestyle is reflected in the beautiful settings and achievements in architecture. The dichotomy in the values of many prominent Americans is also revealed here. Early owners, for the most part, believed their wealth and high position were either the will of God or the natural order of things, despite the fact that they also believed in America's commitment to universal freedom and human dignity.

Trace the path of history and graceful living as you drive southwest. From Baltimore take the Baltimore-Washington Expressway southwest (M–295) to Riverdale Road west. From Riverdale Road west, pick up the East-West Highway west (M–410) to Riverdale in Prince George's County.

The Prince George's Travel Promotion Council welcomes your requests for additional information and recommends the Early Mansions and Aerospace tours described in this day trip.

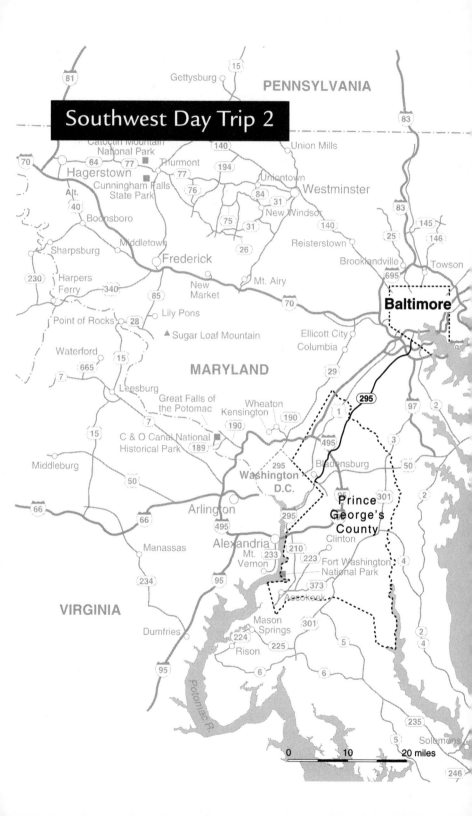

Southwest Day Trip 2

WHERE TO GO

Riversdale (also known as the Calvert Mansion). Located at 4811 Riverdale Road in Riversdale. The mansion is located 2 blocks south of the East-West Highway (M-410) between US-1 and Kenilworth Avenue (M-201); it is a short distance east of the B&O Railroad tracks.

Construction of Riversdale was begun in 1801 by Baron Henri Joseph Stier, a Belgian nobleman who immigrated to America. When the Baron returned to Belgium in 1803, his daughter Rosalie and her husband, George Calvert, moved into the mansion and completed it. Riversdale's unique architectural design combines the functional simplicity of an American plantation home with the interior elegance of a Belgian chateau.

In 1838, Charles Benedict Calvert, the son of George and Rosalie, became proprietor of Riversdale. He was directly responsible for the founding of the Maryland Agricultural College (now the University of Maryland) and was also the prime mover behind the establishment of the U.S. Department of Agriculture. Riversdale remained in the Calvert family until 1887 and later became the home of four members of Congress. Since 1949, it has been owned and maintained by the Maryland-National Capital Park and Planning Commission.

Open for tours. Fee. (301) 864-0420. (While in the area you may want to visit the George Washington House located south of here and included in Day Trip 3 of this sector.)

Montpelier. From Riversdale Mansion, return to the East-West Highway east (M-410) to the Baltimore-Washington Expressway north (M-295) toward Baltimore. Then take M-197 west to Muirkirk Road. Turn left onto Muirkirk Road and immediately right into the Montpelier Mansion driveway.

Montpelier, a masterpiece of Georgian architecture, was built in the 1770s by Major Thomas Snowden. Throughout its long history, Montpelier has had many notable visitors. George Washington was the guest of Major Snowden twice in 1787, as he traveled to and from the Constitutional Convention in Philadelphia. In 1789, Martha Washington was the guest of the Snowdens, as she journeyed to New York for her husband's first inauguration. In 1800, Abigail Adams lodged at Montpelier on her way south to join President John Adams in the "new" White House.

In 1803, Montpelier passed to a descendant, Nicholas Snowden, who in 1824 established a successful cotton mill at the Laurel Factory (now the town of Laurel). The estate remained in the hands of the Snowden family until 1888. Later owners included diplomats and politicians. Since 1961, the property has been owned and maintained by the Maryland-National Capital Park and Planning Commission.

Tours are available. Fee. Call (301) 953-1376 for information.

Belair. Located at 12207 Tulip Grove Drive. From Montpelier, drive east on M-197 toward Bowie for about 10 miles to Tulip Grove Drive (first intersection after junction M-197 and M-450). Turn left on Tulip Grove Drive for about ½ mile to Belair Mansion.

The central block of Belair was built in the 1740s for Provincial Governor Samuel Ogle. It was subsequently the home of his son, Benjamin Ogle, who was an elected governor of Maryland from 1798 to 1801. There was considerable renovation of the interior during the residence of Benjamin Ogle, Jr., the third generation of his family to occupy Belair. It was during this time that the interior of the mansion was finished. He lived here with his large family of fourteen children between 1796 and 1844.

Belair passed out of the Ogle family in 1871 and, after a series of short-term owners, was purchased by James T. Woodward. In the next several years, under the care of the Woodward family, a new series of major renovations was completed, including addition of the two balancing wings. The Woodwards were famous in the thoroughbred horse-racing world. The stables, which housed such famous Belair horses as Nashua, stand a short distance to the east of the mansion. The Belair Mansion is currently owned by the city of Bowie.

Tours are available. No admission fee is charged, but a donation is requested. Call (301) 262-6200 or (301) 805-5029 for information.

Marietta. Located at 5626 Bell Station Road. From Belair Mansion return to Tulip Grove Drive and turn right onto M-197 northwest. At M-450 west turn left for about 2¼ miles to Bell Station Road. Continue on Bell Station Road for about ¼ mile to Marietta Mansion.

Marietta was built by Judge Gabriel Duvall early in the nineteenth century and was his home for the last thirty years of his life. Gabriel Duvall was noted for a lifetime of public service. He served as a member of the Maryland State Legislature and the United States Congress. He was appointed Comptroller of the Treasury by President Jefferson in 1802, a position he held until his appointment to the Supreme Court by President Madison in 1811.

About the time of his appointment to the high court, Duvall began the building of Marietta, a handsome Federal-style brick house, highlighted by stone arches over each window. He added a two-story wing on the north side of the main house in the 1830s.

Duvall retired from the Supreme Court in 1835 and died at Marietta in 1844. The house remained in the possession of his descendants until 1902 and was deeded to the present owner, the Maryland-National Capital Park and Planning Commission, in 1968.

Tours are available. Fee. For information, call (301) 464-5291. From Marietta Mansion return to M–450 east to US–301 north to Baltimore.

If you have more time or would like to design a weekend package, consider taking M–450 east to a short shunt on US–301 north (Crain Highway) and pick up M–450 east again toward Annapolis, Maryland. What is generally a scenic entrance to the state's capital will turn a bit commercial as you arrive at West Street. But drive on, as this route delivers you directly onto Church Circle in the historic district of Annapolis. From Annapolis, you might want to choose some tour options from the day trips listed in the Southeast sector. Or, continue on M–450 west to Bladensburg and Day Trip 3, this section.

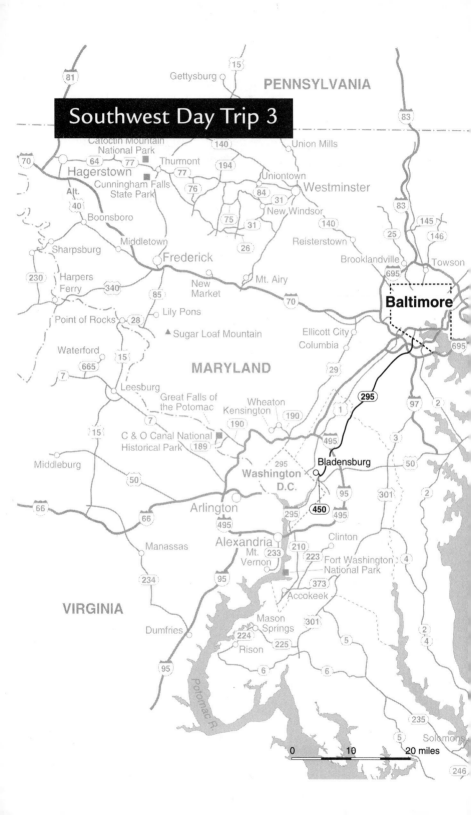

Southwest Day Trip 3

PRINCE GEORGE'S COUNTY, MD

The entire span of American aerospace history is presented in all its richness and color in this day trip to Prince George's County. From the first balloon ascent in America, to the training of the first U.S. Army officers as airplane pilots, to the monitoring of man's journeys to the moon—it all happened here in this tour radius. The coming and going of the world's leaders at Andrews Air Force Base is witness to the continuing aerospace and aviation history-making in this area. The planning, development, and monitoring of American space travel and exploration are taking place at the Goddard Space Flight Center. And, the entire history of flight is represented and preserved in the Smithsonian's Paul E. Garber Facility at Silver Hill.

Begin this day trip for an earthbound tour of a spectrum of aviation. From Baltimore, take the Baltimore-Washington Expressway southwest (M-295) to Bladensburg in Prince George's County. Pick up M-450 west from M-295 to Bladensburg. Visitor information: (301) 925-8300.

WHERE TO GO

The George Washington House. Located at 4302 Baltimore Avenue, Bladensburg. The house stands in the median area between the north- and southbound lanes of Baltimore Avenue, just north of its intersection with M-450.

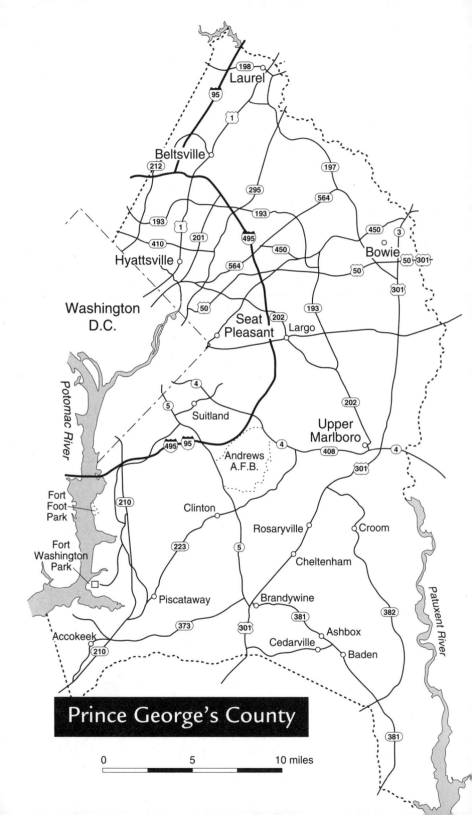

On June 17, 1784, Peter Carnes, a jack-of-all-trades, launched an unmanned hot air balloon in a field adjacent to the town of Bladensburg. This was the first documented unmanned balloon ascent in America. These early experiments were a spectacular success for both Peter Carnes and American aeronautics.

Today, five eighteenth-century buildings survive from the seaport town of Bladensburg that Carnes knew: **Bostwick** (c. 1746); the **Hilleary-Magrudger House** (c. 1745); **Old Clements** (c. 1760); the **Market Master's House** (c. 1764); and the **George Washington House** (c. 1760), which was run as a store by Carnes from 1774 to 1783. None of these buildings are open to the public, but for more information call (301) 925-8300. (While in the area, you might want to slip north to the Riversdale Mansion described in Day Trip 2 of this section.)

College Park Airport and Museum. Located at 6709 Corporal Frank Scott Drive. Travel north on Baltimore Avenue (US-1) for about 2½ miles to Calvert Road. Turn right on Calvert Road and drive east for about ½ mile to Corporal Frank Scott Drive (immediately after the railroad track). Turn left onto Scott Drive to the College Park Airport.

College Park Airport, the "World's Oldest Continuously Operated Airport," has been associated with many of the most important people and events in aviation history. In 1909, Wilbur Wright journeyed to College Park Airport to train the first U.S. military officers to fly an airplane. In October 1909, Lieutenant Frederic H. Humphreys became the first U.S. military officer to pilot an aircraft, and Mrs. Ralph Van Deman became the first woman to fly in an airplane. Later that year, Lieutenant George Sweet became the first naval officer to fly in an airplane.

In the years that followed, many other dramatic aviation firsts occurred at College Park Airport, including: testing of the first bomb-dropping device (1911), the first night landing (1911), the first firing of a machine gun from an airplane in flight (1912), the first controlled helicopter flight (1924), and the first experiments with blind landing equipment and navigational aids (1927–1935). In addition, the airport served as the first regularly scheduled air mail terminus in the United States (1918). College Park continues today as an operating airport and is now owned by the Maryland-National Capital Park and Planning Commission.

Free tours of the airport are available. Tours of the Airport Museum are available. Fee. For information, call (301) 864-6029.

Goddard Space Flight Center. Soil Conservation Road, Greenbelt. From College Park, travel east on Greenbelt Road (M-193) past the entrance to the Baltimore-Washington Parkway and continue on to Soil Conservation Road (½ mile past the main entrance to the Goddard Space Flight Center). Turn left on Soil Conservation Road to the visitors center immediately on the left.

Established in 1959, Goddard Space Flight Center is one of the largest research and development facilities of the National Aeronautics and Space Administration (NASA). It is primarily responsible for the nation's near-Earth satellites; management of the design, development, and construction of spacecraft; and management of the worldwide tracking and communications network for manned and unmanned spacecraft. The center was named in honor of Robert H. Goddard, "Father of American Rocketry." His numerous contributions to this field provided the basis for man's entry into space exploration.

The visitor center at Goddard contains exhibits illustrating NASA programs: the *Delta* rocket mock-up on prominent display outside the museum building; *Mercury, Gemini,* and *Apollo* command modules; a moon rock sample; and an extensive satellite collection. In addition to regular museum hours, the visitor center is host to a model rocket launch for the public several times each month.

Adjoining the area are a convenient snack shop, picnic area, and gift shop. Parking is free. The use of cameras is encouraged.

Tours are available at no charge. For information, call (301) 286-8981.

Paul E. Garber Facility. Silver Hill Road, Silver Hill, MD. Return to M-193 and drive west (right turn) for about 2¼ miles to the Baltimore-Washington Parkway (US-1). Take the Parkway south, toward Washington, then immediately south on I-95 toward Alexandria. Continue on I-95 (Capital Beltway) to exit 11B and drive west on M-4 for 2½ miles to Silver Hill Road (M-458). Turn left on Silver Hill Road for about 2 miles to the intersection of St. Barnabas Road (M-414), and bear right on Old Silver Hill Road. An immediate right will bring you to the parking lot of the Garber Facility.

The Garber Facility at Silver Hill, an adjunct to the National Air and Space Museum (NASM) of the Smithsonian Institution, was established in the mid-1950s as a depository for NASM's reserve collection. This no-frills museum houses many historically significant air- and spacecraft. It is also a storage, restoration, and preservation center. Here, the story of flight history and preservation is told in a simple, realistic setting.

Aircraft of the World War I era are on display, and a fighter plane similar to the one flown by Captain Eddie Rickenbacker gives evidence of the courage and technical skills of early military pilots. The Enola Gay, the B-29 that carried the first atomic bomb to Hiroshima on August 6, 1945, was recently refurbished here before its controversial placement in the Smithsonian Air and Space Museum. In addition, the original nose cone of the Jupiter launch vehicle that carried the first monkeys into space in 1959 and set the precedent for later manned space efforts is also on display here.

Tours are available. Free. For information, call (202) 357-1400.

Andrews Air Force Base. Allentown Road. From the Garber Facility parking lot make an immediate left onto Silver Hill Road (M-458) and drive about 1 mile to Suitland Road. Turn right onto Suitland Road and drive for about 2¾ miles to Allentown Road and the main gate of Andrews Air Force Base.

The base was established in 1942 as Camp Springs Army Airfield by order of President Roosevelt. It was renamed Andrews Air Field in 1945, and in 1947 the facility was designated as Andrews Air Force Base. The base was named in honor of Lieutenant General Frank M. Andrews who, at the time of his death in an aircraft accident in 1943, was commander of all Army Air Force operations in Europe.

Since the end of World War II, Andrews Air Force Base has served as headquarters for the Continental Air Command, Strategic Air Command, Military Air Transport Service, and Air Force Systems Command. During the Korean War it became a combat-readiness training base for B-25 bomber crews. During the Vietnam War, it was the receiving station for medical evacuees, and starting in 1973 it was the homecoming station for prisoners of war.

Tours are only available by appointment. Free. Call (301) 981-4511. (From here you can go straight home by taking the Capital Beltway from Forestville Road and driving northwest back to Baltimore on M-295 north. Or, during warm weather, you might want to take advantage of the water slides or roller coasters at Adventure World in Largo, Maryland.)

Adventure World. Largo. Take exit 15A off the Capital Beltway (I-95) to M-214 east (Central Avenue). Take your bathing suit and challenge the water slides and other attractions. Drier activities include roller coaster rides and other thrill-packed offerings. Adventure World boasts some of the most exciting new thrill rides in the eastern U.S. Fee. ☐. (301) 249-1500.

To return to Baltimore, take Central Avenue west to the Capital Beltway and drive northwest to the Baltimore-Washington Parkway (M-295N) to the city.

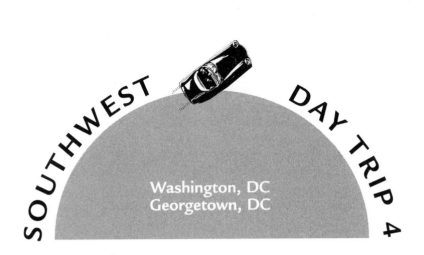

SOUTHWEST DAY TRIP 4

Washington, DC
Georgetown, DC

WASHINGTON, DC

One sure way to begin at the beginning in our nation's capital is to stop at the tourist information center at 1455 Pennsylvania Avenue NW between the Hotel Washington and the Willard Hotel. Located just 1 block from the White House, the center provides free maps, brochures, and touring suggestions. It is open daily from 9:00 A.M. to 5:00 P.M. or call ahead for information at (202) 789-7000. In addition, twenty-four-hour recorded visitor information on events and happenings is available from the Washington Convention and Visitors Association's Dial-an-Event line at (202) 737-8866.

From the tourist information center, day trip drivers may wish to take an escorted driving tour of the city's attractions in order to get an overall perspective. Narrated shuttle tours to major sites in and around Washington offer unlimited free reboarding, so you can visit sites at your own pace. Tickets may be purchased from the Tourmobile drivers at designated stops along the National Mall. This federal park extends from the Capitol Building grounds on the east to the Lincoln Memorial on the west between Madison and Jefferson Streets. For more information regarding the Tourmobiles, call (202) 554-7950.

For general geographic orientation, here's some information that may help you get around. The U.S. Capitol Building, at the east end of the Mall, is the hub of Washington's streets. The Capitol is located at the intersection of East Capitol Street, South Capitol Street, North Capitol Street, and the Mall, in lieu of a "West Capitol." The

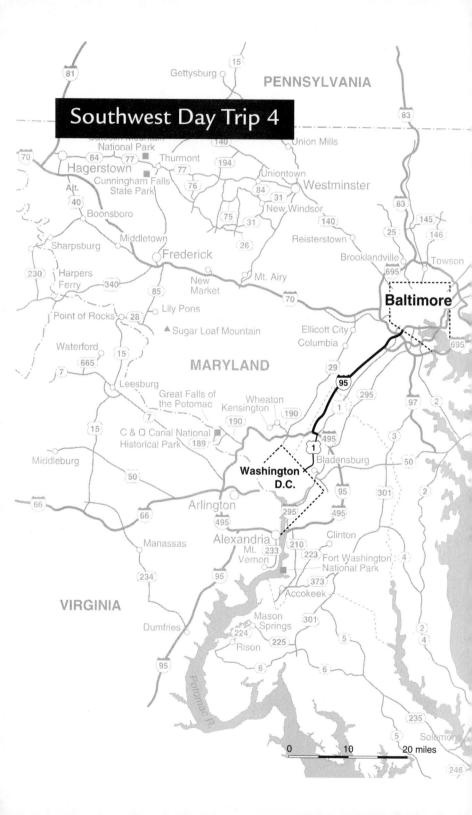

Southwest Day Trip 4

three streets and the Mall divide the city into quadrants: Northeast, Northwest, Southeast, and Southwest.

All numbered streets run north and south. Lettered streets run east and west. Streets with state names, such as Pennsylvania, are diagonals, with the White House as the geographic center of Washington's original 10-mile square.

There are more than one hundred points of interest in and around the area, along with numerous theaters and cultural opportunities. It is best to write in advance and get information you'll need to make your day trip more enjoyable. Your requests are welcome at the Washington, DC, Convention and Visitors Association, 1212 New York Avenue NW, Washington, DC 20005. (202) 789-7000. In the meantime, here are a few of the delights to be sampled in the area.

WHERE TO GO

U.S. Capitol Building. Intersection of East Capitol Street, South Capitol Street, North Capitol Street, and the Mall. In 1793, George Washington officiated at the laying of the cornerstone, but it wasn't completed until 1807, although in 1800 President John Adams insisted that the first sessions be held there. Explore the cradle of our country's politics. Its famous 180-foot white dome presides over the Rotunda and the adjoining House of Representatives and the Senate. Visitors are invited to hear debates on the floor of the House or Senate. Passes to the galleries may be obtained for U.S. citizens from their state senators or representatives.

Foreign visitors should apply to the office of the Sergeant at Arms of the Senate. Free tours of the Rotunda, Statuary Hall (with two statues from each state), the House of Representatives (the largest legislative chamber in the world), the Senate (with its famous reception room), and the Crypt (the original site of the Supreme Court) are designed for about thirty to forty minutes of touring time. Open daily for tours except Thanksgiving, Christmas, and New Year's Day. (202) 225-6827.

Washington Monument. East end of the National Mall at 15th Street. Dedicated in 1885 to the memory of our first U.S. president, this 555-foot obelisk is the world's largest masonry structure. Adventurous visitors may enjoy the panoramic view from atop its observation area. The elevator whisks you to the top in a seventy-second trip. If you'd like to walk down, the National Park Service conducts Walking Down Step Tours on weekends to explain the 188 memorial stones that were donated for the interior walls. Open daily. Free. (202) 426-6839.

Lincoln Memorial. West Potomac Park and 23rd Street NW. Looking west across 17th Street, the peaceful beauty of the Reflecting Pool gives way to the Grecian-like temple that is a monument to our sixteenth president. The 19-foot statue of Abraham Lincoln is as inspiring to visitors as the words from his speeches that are carved in the surrounding walls. The western view from the Memorial encompasses the Potomac River and the Arlington National Cemetery on its western bank. Famous American sculptor Daniel Chester French designed the Brooding Lincoln statue and supervised the actual carving, which took four years to complete, from twenty-eight blocks of Georgia white marble. Free. (202) 426-6895.

Vietnam Veterans Memorial. Constitution Avenue between Henry Bacon Drive and 21st Street NW. This modern V-shaped memorial designed by Maya Ying Lin is inscribed with the names of the 58,156 people who died or remain missing in the Vietnam War. Large books are available to help locate the names on the walls. A directory listing the inscribed names can be purchased. Call (202) 347-2054. A guard is on duty from 8:00 A.M. until midnight daily. Free. (202) 634-1568.

Jefferson Memorial. Tidal Basin (South Bank), West Potomac Park. Dedicated in 1943 to the memory of President Thomas Jefferson, the classical Greek dome and colonnade is in the style he most preferred. Inside is a 19-foot bronze statue beneath a simple rotunda. The walls are filled with quotations from the Declaration of Independence and other Jefferson writings. Open daily. Free.

John F. Kennedy Center for the Performing Arts. New Hampshire Avenue at Rock Creek Parkway. Drama, dance, music, and film are presented here. This Center is the home of the National Symphony, the Washington Opera, and the American Film Institute. Programs and services for children and the disabled are available. Free tours daily. (202) 416-8000. Tickets, (202) 467-4600.

The Ellipse. Looking north from the Washington Monument at the National Mall, just beyond Constitution Avenue. This comely, flowered park is a favorite spot of quiet and solitude for nearby office workers and visitors. At the northern edge is Pennsylvania Av-

enue NW and the White House.

The White House. Located at 1600 Pennsylvania Avenue NW. This has been the home of every U.S. president since 1800. Eight to nine rooms of the 132-room mansion are open for tours. The wait for tickets can be long and the tours can be as short as ten minutes. If you are intent upon a personal tour, contact your senator or congressperson—about six months in advance if possible—and request a Congressional Early Morning Tour, which will take place between 7:45 and 9:45 A.M. and will last about thirty minutes. Open Tuesday through Saturday. Closed Christmas, New Year's Day, and during presidential functions. Free. (202) 208-1631.

The National Gallery of Art. Fourth Street and Constitution Avenue NW. The gallery features extensive collections of European and American works. The collection is so extensive, it must be seen and cannot be adequately described in such little space as is available here. (202) 737-4215.

The Smithsonian Institution Museum Group. On the Mall between Constitution Avenue to the north and Independence Avenue to the south. Included within these walls are many important collections.

The Museum of Natural History. Located at 10th and Constitution Avenue NW, this museum contains collections of fellow earth inhabitants ranging from the far corners of the globe and prehistoric eras.

The National Air and Space Museum. Located at 6th Street and Independence Avenue NW, this museum features the history of aviation from the original aircraft of the Wright brothers to Charles Lindbergh's *Spirit of St. Louis,* Amelia Earhart's *Vega,* and the 1986 *Voyager,* a lightweight flying fuel tank that circumnavigated the globe nonstop, to present-day, state-of-the-art satellites and rockets. The IMAX Theatre runs some of the very best mammoth screen aviation productions.

The Hirshhorn Museum and Sculpture Garden. Located at 8th Street and Independence Avenue NW, the Hirshhorn displays an astounding collection of nineteenth- and twentieth-century art, including works of Matisse, Picasso, and Rodin.

General visitor information regarding the Smithsonian Group may be obtained by calling (202) 357-2700, 9:00 A.M. to 5:00 P.M. daily. Recorded event information is available at (202) 357-3235. Information may also be obtained through the visitor information center in the newly remodeled Castle Building, which offers an excellent overview of the Smithsonian Institution.

United States Holocaust Memorial Museum. Located at 100 Raoul Wallenberg Place, between Independence Avenue and D Street SW. This truly inspiring museum is one of Washington's newest. Opened in 1993, the museum exhibits are not the only experience that you'll find here. The entire atmosphere is one of reality and participation. As you enter, you'll be given a computer card with a victim's name and history. At various points along the tour, you'll be able to put the card into a machine that will update the victim's fate, to that point. One does not need to be Jewish to be deeply touched by this experience. The museum is free but the volume of visitors has been overwhelming, so you might want to seek reservations. (202) 488-0400.

Note: Most galleries and museums do have a fee; call for details.

GEORGETOWN, DC

While in Washington, be sure to visit Georgetown, which is located mainly along M Street and Wisconsin Avenue in the Southwest sector of the city. Numerous small shops feature excellent glassware, wood, fabrics, clothing, and books.

More opportunities abound in **Georgetown Park,** a Victorian-style edifice that occupies a square block between M Street and the C&O Canal. Within the elaborately decorated, three-tiered building are a variety of restaurants and specialty shops ranging from reasonable to expensive.

Georgetown's **M Street** features some of the best entertainment in Washington. Excellent jazz and live stand-up comedy are profiled against the pomp and grandeur of the nation's capital. Dining spots are plentiful. From the creative concoctions of the natural food store, to the hearty fare of the popular pubs, to the elegant offerings of the Georgetown Inn, it's all here for your pleasure.

Many of the other destinations listed in the day trips of the Southwest sector would make excellent adjuncts to this tour if you want to design an itinerary beyond the two-hour guidelines.

From Washington, select New York Avenue northbound to leave the city. This road becomes the Baltimore-Washington Parkway (M–295) and will lead you directly back to Baltimore.

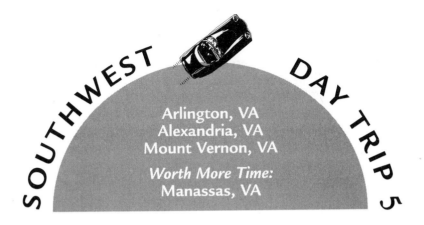

Arlington, VA
Alexandria, VA
Mount Vernon, VA

Worth More Time:
Manassas, VA

ARLINGTON, VA

Situated on the south bank of the Potomac River is the second
smallest county in the United States. Arlington, a suburb of Washington, DC, was developed over approximately 25 square miles of
the northern tip of Virginia. In 1847, the federal government de-
cided it would never need the space for further Washington development, so the land was ceded back to Virginia. From Baltimore
take US–40 west to US–29 south to Washington. In Washington
continue south on US–29, which is New Hampshire Avenue.
Follow it around Washington Circle to pick up US–240 southeast
(23rd Street) to the Lincoln Memorial. From the Lincoln Memorial
pick up the Arlington Memorial Bridge into the Arlington National Cemetery.

WHERE TO GO

Arlington National Cemetery. Located on the Virginia side of the
Arlington Memorial Bridge. Established in 1864, Arlington is the
best known of all the national cemeteries. The ownership of the original parcel of land upon which the cemetery was developed is traced
back to George Washington. Through a network of marriages and
inheritances, it became the property of Robert E. Lee. The 612 acres
of rolling lands dotted with simple headstones, virtually as far as the
eye can see, bear silent witness to the futility of war and the wages of
conducting them.

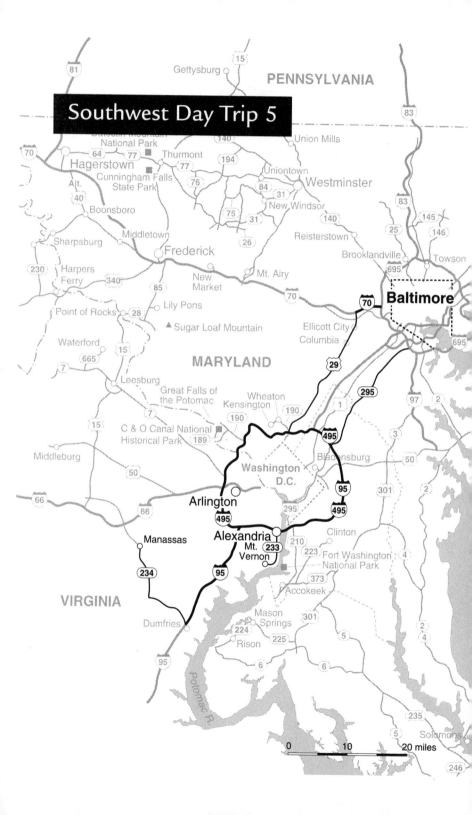

For many people, a visit to this national landmark is an opportunity to pay personal respects to the soldiers of the Tomb of the Unknowns and the graves of President John F. Kennedy and Senator Robert F. Kennedy. President Kennedy's grave is marked by an eternal flame and quotations from his inaugural address. Nearby are the graves of his two infant children. The Tomb of the Unknowns is guarded twenty-four hours a day by the "Old Guard" Third U.S. Infantry Regiment. A precision ceremony of the changing of the guard takes place every half-hour in the daytime from April through the end of September, every hour for the remainder of the year, and every two hours at night.

Buried in the National Cemetery are George Washington Parke Custis and Mrs. Custis, Pierre L'Enfant, William Howard Taft, General John J. Pershing, Robert E. Peary, Rear Admiral Richard E. Byrd, John Foster Dulles, and many other famous Americans. More than a quarter-million people are buried here—representing the American Revolution, the Civil War, Spanish-American War, World Wars I and II, and the conflicts in Korea, Vietnam, and the Persian Gulf.

The cemetery is open daily, year-round. Parking is at the visitors center on Eisenhower Drive where special passes are distributed to family members and friends of those buried here. Otherwise, for the general public, Tourmobiles leave the visitors center for regularly scheduled narrated tours of the major points of interest. Parking fee. (703) 692-0931.

Arlington House. Just above the cemetery as you enter from the Arlington Memorial Bridge sits the house of Robert E. Lee and his bride, Mary Anna Rudolph Custis. The building was begun in 1802 by George Washington Parke Custis, grandson of Martha Washington. The Lees occupied the house from 1831 to 1861. It was here, in 1861, that Lee made his fateful decision to resign his commission in the U.S. Army in order to defend his native state. When Lee was attending to the Confederate troops in Richmond, Union forces occupied the house, because of its position, which commanded approaches to Washington. They buried their dead on the slopes beneath it.

The property was confiscated by the government in 1864 due to nonpayment of taxes. A Lee descendant sued for the return of the property and won. By then, however, thousands of graves covered the estate and the property was sold back to the government for

$150,000. Now administered by the National Park Service, the mansion is being restored to its 1861 appearance along with the return of some of the original furnishings of the Custis and Lee families. Open for tours. Free. (703) 557–0613.

United States Marine Corps War Memorial. Arlington Boulevard at Meade Street, Rosslyn. North of Arlington National Cemetery. The Iwo Jima Memorial is the re-creation of Joseph Rosenthal's Pulitzer Prize–winning photo of the flag raising atop Mt. Suribachi. The hundred-ton sculpture is 78 feet high.

ALEXANDRIA, VA

Alexandria, a seaport town with a rich maritime and trading heritage, is located on the Potomac River across from Washington, DC. It was founded by Scottish merchants in 1749, and clipper ships brought a booming tobacco trade here to the Potomac River shores. Alexandria was one of George Washington's favorite cities. He attended church here and drilled his soldiers in preparation for the nation's first fight for freedom.

Today Alexandria boasts 108,000 residents and more than one million visitors annually. Tradition lives in the city's historic homes, churches, and taverns beautifully preserved like a colonial sampler. The rich heritage and colorful past live also in the many specialty shops and art galleries housed in restored eighteenth- and nineteenth-century buildings.

In this veritable melting pot of nationalities, excellent restaurants feature French, Greek, Afghan, Scottish, Italian, Creole, and (ah, yes!) traditional American colonial fare.

Alexandria could be a single-destination day trip if you prefer. It lends itself beautifully to a walking tour, which is described below. Many historic sites are within a stroll of one another. Shopping is particularly interesting and colorful, and the day trip visitor can top off the tour with a variety of choices for dining. To see the town at its best, consult the Alexandria Convention and Visitors Bureau, which recommends a walking tour of the sites listed below.

From Baltimore take the Baltimore-Washington Expressway (M-295) toward Washington. Then, pick up the Capital Beltway southeast (I-95, alternately designated I-495) and drive to US-1 north into Alexandria. Enter Alexandria on Patrick Street (US-1N), turn right onto Franklin Street, then left onto Fairfax Street, and continue until you reach the intersection of Fairfax and King Streets. Or, if you plan to travel from Arlington, take Henry G. Shirley Memorial Highway south to Alexandria.

WHERE TO GO

The Ramsay House. Located at 221 King Street. Your first stop on a tour of Alexandria should be the Ramsay House. Now the official visitors center, it is a reconstruction of the original house, which was built around 1724 and moved by barge upriver to its present resting site after Alexandria was established in 1749. William Ramsay, Alexandria's first postmaster, was a Scottish merchant and city founder. Today this site houses a restaurant, hotel, gallery, and shops. It features video, walking, and trolley tours and foreign translations in nineteen languages. The offices of the Alexandria Convention and Visitors Bureau are also located here. Open daily. Free. (703) 838-4200 or (800) 388-9119.

The Old Presbyterian Meeting House. Located at 321 South Fairfax Street. Built in 1774 by Scottish founders of Alexandria, the Meeting House served as a gathering place for patriots.

George Washington's funeral sermons were preached here in 1799 when bad weather made roads to Christ Church impassable. The graveyard is the site of the Tomb of the Unknown Soldier of the American Revolution and of grave markers for Colonel Dennis Ramsay and other esteemed Alexandrians. Open for tours. Free. (703) 549-6670.

The Torpedo Factory Art Center. Located at 105 North Union Street. The Art Center houses the studios of nearly 200 professional artists and craftsmen who create and sell on the premises. Originally a torpedo shell case factory built in 1918, the Art Center is an imaginative example of adaptive re-use. Free. (703) 838-4565.

Alexandria Archeology. Located at 105 North Union Street. This program is one of the few such American research facilities devoted to the conservation of sites in an urban development. The city-operated laboratory and exhibit area are located in the Torpedo Factory. Free. (703) 838-4399.

The Carlyle House. Located at 121 North Fairfax Street. Alexandria's grandest home was built in 1752 by the Scottish merchant

John Carlyle. Design of the Carlyle House was thought to be inspired by Craigiehall, an imposing stone manor house in Scotland. In the spring of 1755, General Edward Braddock made Carlyle House his Alexandria headquarters. At a meeting in the home's elegant great parlor, Braddock and five colonial governors planned the strategy and funding of the early campaigns of the French and Indian War. Open for tours. Fee. (703) 549-2997.

Market Square. Located at 300 block of King Street. In 1749, two half-acre lots were set aside during the survey of the city for a marketplace and town hall, which was constructed in 1752. Over the years, schools, jails, whipping posts, private fire companies, and, in 1817, a bell and clock tower were added. After a fire in 1871, a U-shaped Victorian building with its front on Cameron Street and two wings along Fairfax and Royal Streets was built with a central courtyard that housed the market. An addition in 1962 has closed the U, but the market, the oldest continuously operating market in the country, is still held early on Saturday mornings. (703) 838-4000.

Gadsby's Tavern Museum. Located at 134 North Royal Street. Known for its outstanding Georgian architecture, Gadsby's Tavern Museum consists of two important buildings built around 1770 and 1792. The tavern was a center of political, business, and social life in early Alexandria. Celebrations honoring George Washington were held in the second-floor ballroom to music played from a musicians gallery. Open for tours. Fee. (703) 838-4242.

Boyhood Home of Robert E. Lee. Located at 607 Oronoco Street, between Washington and St. Asaph Streets, "Light Horse Harry" Lee, Revolutionary War hero and father of Robert E. Lee, brought his family to this house in 1812. Lee lived and studied here in his early childhood years. The preserved house is beautifully furnished with rare antiques and Lee memorabilia. Open for tours. Fee. (703) 548-8454.

Lee-Fendall House. Located at 614 Oronoco Street. A long line of Lees lived in and visited this rambling wooden structure built in 1789 by Philip Fendall. He was a member of a prominent Charles County, Maryland, family and had three wives, all Lee women. In this house, "Light Horse Harry" wrote the farewell address from the citizens of Alexandria when Washington left Mount Vernon to become the first president of the United States. Open for tours. Fee. (703) 548-1789.

The Lloyd House. Located at 220 North Washington Street, at Queen Street. One of Alexandria's finest examples of late-Georgian architecture, the Lloyd House was built in 1797. Known for its association with the Lee family, the house was purchased in 1832 by John Lloyd, whose wife Anne Harriotte Lee was a cousin of Robert E. Lee. It was owned by the Lloyd family until 1918. Restored for adaptive use in 1976, the building is now part of the Alexandria Library and houses an extensive collection of rare books, records, and documents on city and Virginia history. Open to the public. Free. (703) 838-4577.

Christ Church. Cameron and North Washington Streets. This English country-style church was built between 1767 and 1773 of native brick and stone. George Washington was a member of the vestry; the church contains his family pew. Robert E. Lee was confirmed here and later attended from Arlington House. Winston Churchill and President Franklin Roosevelt attended services here together. Open to the public. Donations accepted. (703) 549-1450.

The Lyceum. Located at 201 South Washington Street at Prince Street. This example of Greek Revival architecture was built in 1839 as a cultural center for Alexandria. In 1974, it was restored and became the nation's first Bicentennial Center. Today it is a museum and center for the comprehensive history of Alexandria. Free. Educational tours arranged. Gift shop on the premises. (703) 838-4994.

The George Washington Masonic National Memorial. King Street and Callahan Drive. The memorial contains outstanding Washington memorabilia, including the family Bible and a clock that was stopped at the time of his death. Large murals and stained-glass windows depict events of Washington's life. Free. (703) 683-2007.

Fort Ward Museum and Historic Site. Located at 4301 West Braddock Road. Owned and operated by the city of Alexandria, Fort Ward is the only Union fort in the defenses of Washington developed as a major Civil War site. The reconstructed museum contains one of the finest collections of Civil War objects. The forty-five-acre park includes a restored bastion, outdoor amphitheater, and picnic facilities. Free. (703) 838-4848.

Black History Resource Center. Located at 638 North Alfred Street (entrance on Wythe Street). This building was constructed in 1940 to house the Robinson Library, the black community's first public library. Dedicated in 1983, this building now serves as a museum documenting the history and accomplishments of blacks in Alexandria and Virginia from 1749 to the present. Paintings, photographs, books, and other memorabilia relate the black experience in Virginia during these eras. Free. (703) 838-4356.

The Alexandria Waterfront Museum. Located at 44 Canal Center Plaza, TransPotomac Canal. Located adjacent to the Tide Lock of the once-prosperous Alexandria Canal, this museum interprets the development of the waterfront and maritime activities from the founding of Alexandria in 1749. Changing exhibitions reflect the history and social life along Alexandria's waterfront in the eighteenth and nineteenth centuries. Visitors may make an appointment to view an archive of canal books, slides, and prints. Free. (703) 838-4288.

MOUNT VERNON, VA

Travel south along the scenic Potomac River toward the historic beauty of Mount Vernon. No wonder George Washington selected this territory for his estate. "No estate in United America is more pleasantly situated," said Washington. The broad sweep of the Potomac, pastoral fields, and beautifully forested areas easily lend themselves to the traditional colonial Virginia lifestyle. From Alexandria follow the Mount Vernon Memorial Highway south (V–233) (also designated the George Washington Parkway) along the shores of the Potomac River to Mount Vernon.

WHERE TO GO

Mount Vernon. Follow V–233 south to its terminus at V–235 west and north, 8 miles south of Alexandria. The exhibition area contains more than thirty acres with several miles of walks and lanes for the visitor to explore. The mansion is, of course, the focal point of any visit to Mount Vernon. Designed and enlarged from the one-and-a-half-story farmhouse of his youth by George Washington, the mansion is a unique and beautiful example of mid-Georgian architecture. Fourteen rooms are shown, which exhibit numerous original furnishings that have been returned through gift, loan, and purchase since 1858. In that year, the nucleus of the estate was purchased from

Washington heirs by the Mount Vernon Ladies' Association in a pioneering example of historic preservation.

Close to the mansion are the north and south service lanes where small, white wooden buildings accommodated the domestic servants and cottage industries that helped sustain the economy of this successful plantation. Nine outbuildings are furnished and open, in addition to the museum on the North Lane with its large collection of silver, porcelain, military equipment, and more. In the nearby brick greenhouse and slave quarters building is a small museum that helps explain the architectural development and restoration of the mansion.

The colonnades lead from the mansion on the west to the kitchen and former servants hall. The two-story piazza on the east allows a view of the mile-wide Potomac River. The rural character of the Maryland shore beyond is now preserved as a National Park, ensuring that the majestic view so enjoyed by the Washingtons and visitors for two centuries will remain unchanged for future generations to enjoy. Open daily. Fee. (703) 780-2000.

Woodlawn Plantation. From Mount Vernon continue west on V-235 to US-1 and the site of Woodlawn Plantation. The rich heritage of northern Virginia is epitomized by this property, once part of George Washington's Dogue Run Farm. The retired president gave the estate to his adopted daughter, Eleanor Parke Custis, and his nephew Lawrence Lewis as a wedding gift. The couple then commissioned Dr. William Thornton, architect of the U.S. Capitol, to design the Georgian mansion. Today it is a property of the National Trust for Historic Preservation, and thousands of visitors enjoy the stately restored mansion with its Federal-style rooms and its broad vista of the Potomac River. Open daily for tours with the exception of Christmas, New Year's Day, and Thanksgiving. Fee. (703) 780-4000.

Continue on US-1 south past **Pohick Church** at Telegraph and Old Colchester Roads. This landmark along the way to Gunston Hall is an Anglican church designed in 1774 by James Wren under the advisement of George Washington. It is open to the public and listed on the National Register of Historic Sites. Free. At V-242 east turn left and arrive at Gunston Hall.

Gunston Hall. Located at 10709 Gunston Road, Lorton. George Mason, Father of the Bill of Rights, created this magnificent Georgian home overlooking the Potomac River near Mount Vernon. Mason's colonial plantation home was complete with outbuildings, extensive formal gardens, and even a deer park. It was a self-sufficient plantation and consisted of more than 5,000 acres devoted to growing wheat and tobacco and grazing sheep. Tiny village-like compounds on the grounds provided housing for craftsmen, servants, and slaves who lived there with their families.

The house was designed and begun before 1755, and Mason called upon the renowned William Buckland to give it the finishing architectural touches and to design the superb carvings as Buckland would later do in many other fine homes of Virginia and Maryland. Fee. (703) 550-9220.

From Gunston Hall, return on V-242 west to US-1 north toward Alexandria for an alternate route. Then pick up I-495 east around Washington on the Capital Beltway to the Baltimore-Washington Parkway north (M-295) for return routing to Baltimore, or continue on to Manassas, if time permits.

WORTH MORE TIME

MANASSAS, VA

Although it is more than two hours from Baltimore, Manassas, Virginia, is a "must do" for American history and Civil War buffs. Manassas set the stage for the first major encounter in the War Between the States. Houses and architecture reflect the Victorian design that was the style when the town was chartered in 1873.

Historic Manassas Inc. Located at 9025 Center Street, Manassas. Call (703) 361-6599 or visit the Manassas Welcome Center, Virginia Division of Tourism, I-66 between US-29 and V-234. From Gunston Hall continue on US-1 south to Dumfries, Virginia. Then pick up V-234 west (Dumfries Road) into Manassas.

WHERE TO GO

Manassas Museum. Located at 9101 Prince William Street. Civil War artifacts, railroading, walking, driving, and architectural tours, local memorabilia, and rotating collections are among the exhibitions. Fee. (703) 368-1873.

Manassas National Battlefield. The park visitor center is located on V-234 between I-66 and US-29 at 6511 Sudley Road. Two great battles of the Civil War—the First and Second Battles of Manassas, also known as the battles of Bull Run—were fought here. It was on this battlefield that General Thomas J. Jackson earned the nickname of "Stonewall Jackson" for standing firm against the Union forces.

The visitor center contains a museum, a slide program, and a battle map. Free. Call (703) 361-7075.

Return routing is begun on V-234 east toward Dumfries. Then pick up US-1 north toward Alexandria and follow the recommended directions to Baltimore listed at the conclusion of Gunston Hall in this section.

WHERE TO STAY

Best Western Manassas. Located at 8640 Mathis Avenue. Located near Breeden Avenue and V-234, Manassas. This newly renovated property is convenient to the battlefield, Skyline Drive, Luray Caverns, and the Potomac Mills Outlets. $$; ☐. (703) 368-7070.

Olde Towne Inn of Manassas. Located at 9405 Main Street. I-66 exit 47A, V-234 south to left on Center Street. This is the only hotel in Historic Old Towne. Coffee house, outdoor pool, walk to most sites. $$; ☐. (703) 368-9191.

WHERE TO EAT

Brady's Public House. Located at 8971 Center Street, Manassas. Relaxing Irish-American atmosphere. Light fare, soup, and sandwiches for lunch. $-$$; ☐. (703) 369-1469.

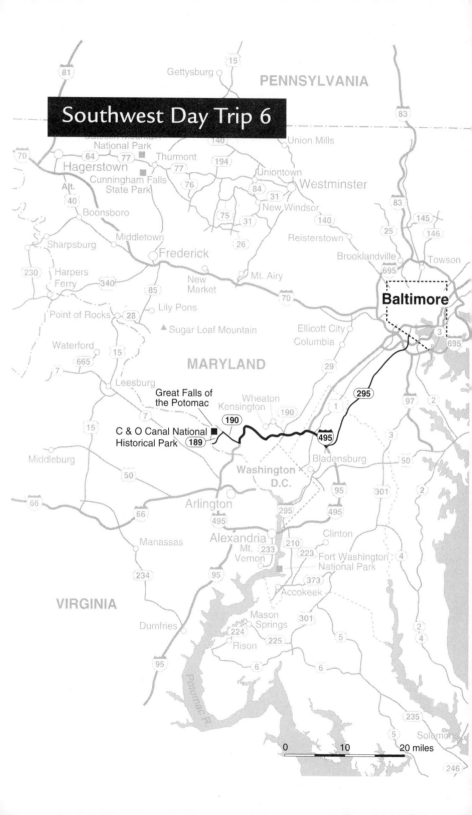

GREAT FALLS OF THE POTOMAC, MD

About 15 miles northwest of Washington, DC, is a series of picturesque falls and rapids. Here the Potomac River roars through a rocky cataract, dropping more than 50 feet to a narrow gorge.

From Baltimore take the Baltimore-Washington Expressway south (M–295) to the Capital Beltway west (I–495) to exit 41 at Carderock, Great Falls, MD. Keep right off ramp onto Clara Barton Memorial Parkway. Follow this parkway to its end, then make a left onto MacArthur Boulevard. While this may seem to be a fast-track start to an otherwise peaceful day, this routing avoids some of the snarls of the Washington suburbs. Take MacArthur Boulevard west to Great Falls. Call (703) 285–2965.

WHERE TO GO

Glen Echo Park. MacArthur Boulevard, near Oxford Road. This land has been utilized for special purposes since 1891, when a National Chautauqua Assembly was established as a center where people could participate in the sciences, arts, languages, and literature. In 1899, it was converted into a full-fledged amusement park. Today it emphasizes arts and cultural education for the community. Visitors can get a good introduction to Glen Echo Park by stopping at the "stone tower" gallery and visiting the workshops of artists located on the premises. Also offered are periodic concerts, demonstrations, workshops, and festivals. An antique, hand-carved Dentzel

Carousel, once a part of the original amusement park, operates on certain days. Call in advance to check on specific information regarding events. (301) 492-6282.

Clara Barton National Historic Site. Located at 5801 Oxford Road near Glen Echo Park. Clara Barton, humanitarian and founder of the American Red Cross, lived in this house for the last fifteen years of her life. Beforehand, this building had been used as a Red Cross warehouse. This beloved home of the persevering woman reflects her personality, giving visitors the opportunity to learn more about her. Free. (301) 492-6245.

C&O CANAL NATIONAL HISTORICAL PARK, MD

Pack your picnic cooler and wear your hiking shoes and comfortable clothing for this trip to the C&O Canal. Get ready for a nature-loving departure from sophisticated shopping and stately mansions. Enjoy your favorite form of getting next to nature: walking, biking, hiking, or camping.

Beginning at the Maryland side of the Potomac River in Georgetown, the canal extends for 184 miles to Cumberland, Maryland. Along the way it passes many sites of natural beauty and historical value. Locks and lockhouses, dams, aqueducts, mule barns, and remnants of once-thriving communities remind us of almost a century of active canal traffic. The canal was begun in 1828 with a dedication by President John Quincy Adams and was proclaimed a National Monument in 1960 by President Dwight Eisenhower.

To compensate for the difference in elevation from Washington to Cumberland and to ensure smooth waters in the canal, seventy-four lift locks were built. Initially each lock was known by a number, but as individual lockkeepers became well known, their names were used for identification, as in Swains Lock and Pennyfield Lock.

Because locking barge through traffic was a day and night operation, lockhouses were built by the canal company to house the lockkeepers and their families. It was also necessary to build aqueducts to carry the canal above the numerous tributaries that flow into the Potomac River. These impressive structures were major engineering accomplishments in their time.

From the visitors center at Great Falls Tavern on the C&O Canal, drive east on MacArthur Boulevard to Falls Road and turn left. Drive northeast on Falls Road to M-190 and turn left. Continue west on M-190 to points of interest in the park.

WHERE TO GO

C&O Canal Museum. Located at 11710 MacArthur Boulevard. Built in 1828 as an inn and lockhouse, Crommelin House (Great Falls Tavern) soon developed a reputation for hospitality along the great canal. Today that tradition lives at the visitors center and museum located here. The museum features a scale model of a boat going through a lock and the canal. Other exhibits include a history of the canal. Fee to enter park. (301) 299-3613.

C&O Trips. Available from the visitors center located at the Great Falls Tavern, these one-and-one-half-hour tours of the canal are conducted aboard a mule-drawn, nineteenth-century-style barge. This living history lesson is given by costumed guides and includes performances of typical tasks of the era and a presentation of period music. Trips also originate in Georgetown at the landing between Thomas Jefferson and 30th Streets. Fee. For information on schedules and charges, call (301) 299-3613.

Swains Lock. Also designated Lock #21, this lock is just west of the Great Falls Tavern on M-190. Picnic facilities, drinking water, and overnight camping are available. For specific information call the Great Falls Tavern. (301) 299-3613.

Pennyfield Lock. Also designated Lock #22, it is located 3 miles west on M-190 from Swains Lock. Here are particularly nice picnic facilities for the day trip visitor. Plan to have your picnic lunch here or continue to Seneca.

Seneca. A bit farther west on M-190, just past Lock #23 (Violets Lock), is Seneca, which offers picnic facilities and a boat ramp. For specific boating information, call the Great Falls Tavern. (301) 299-3613.

The C&O Canal route offers many such stops with conveniences ranging from picnic facilities to drive-in and group camping areas. Information centers and campfire programs are also offered. For points west of Seneca and for general park information, call (301) 739-4200 or write the Park Superintendent, C&O Canal National Historical Park, Box 4, Sharpsburg, MD 21782.

WHAT TO DO

Canoeing. Canoeing on short and widely separated stretches of the canal is a popular recreation in the park. Maps helpful to the visitor can be obtained by writing the U.S. Geological Survey, Branch of Distribution, 1200 Eads Street, Arlington, VA 22202, or by calling (703) 557-2751. The U.S. Weather Bureau provides a telephone message for those interested in river conditions in the lower Potomac Valley. (202) 899-3210.

Cycling. Many cyclists enjoy the towpath on the canal. Ambitious travelers tackle the entire 184 miles between Cumberland and Georgetown. Others are content with shorter outings. Three sections lend themselves to one-day bike trips. The towpath in these areas is in good condition and the scenery is great! These areas include: Great Falls Tavern to Georgetown, 14 miles; Fifteen Mile Creek to Paw Paw Tunnel, 15 miles; and Dam 4 to Lock #33, 24 miles. There is access by motor vehicle to either end of these areas.

Be sure to contact the park superintendent as previously listed for general maps and timely detour information. (301) 739-4200.

Fishing. Fishing has long been one of the most popular activities for visitors to the park. The Potomac contains a number of game species, including bass, catfish, carp, sunfish, and shad. Areas recommended for fishing are North Branch, Oldtown, Seneca, Big Pool, and Little Pool. For specific information regarding regulations and other details, obtain the latest Maryland Sportfishing Guide by contacting the Information Division, Department of Natural Resources, Tawes State Office Building, Annapolis, MD 21401. Park rangers on patrol are also knowledgeable resources for this information.

Camping. All campsites are on a first-come, first-served basis except Marsden Tract, which must be reserved ahead. (301) 299-3613.

Stay is limited to fourteen days at the drive-in areas, ten days at the "carry-in," and one night at each hiker-biker area per trip. Conveniences, facilities, and regulations will vary with each site, so write or phone ahead to the park superintendent, as previously described, for details.

Return to Baltimore via M-190 east to the Capital Beltway east (I-495). Then pick up the Baltimore-Washington Parkway north (M-295) to Baltimore.

If you're planning an overnight trip, you may want to select some of the destinations described in the day trips of the Western sector in the following chapter. The carefully selected secondary roads described in that sector's day trips will take you on a scenic route to Harpers Ferry, West Virginia, and Antietam, Maryland, among other such attractions.

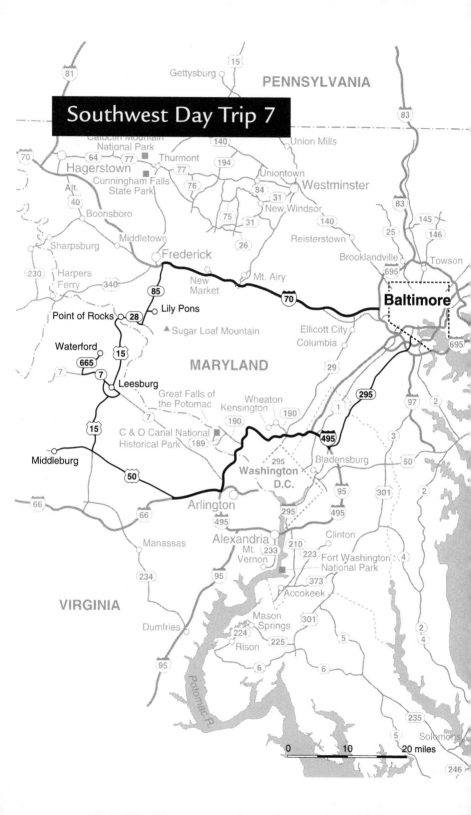

Southwest Day Trip 7

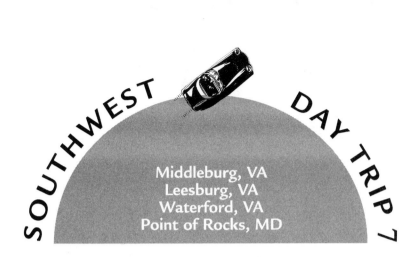

MIDDLEBURG, VA

The unofficial capital of the "Hunt Country" of Virginia, Middle-burg was first known as an overnight stagecoach stop with its convenient location midway between Alexandria and Winchester. Today many visitors are attracted to this picturesque little community and the many Hunt Country events. Such activities as the Glenwood Steeplechase and Carriage Drive in the spring, the Loudoun Junior and Pony Show in June, and the Middleburg Wine Festival in autumn proudly show off the best of this beautiful wine and horse country. Unique shops and delightful restaurants make Middleburg an enjoyable place to visit.

From Baltimore take the Baltimore-Washington Expressway south (M-295) to the Capital Beltway west (I-495) to US-50 west into Middleburg.

Meredyth Vineyards. From US-50 at Middleburg take V-776 south for 2½ miles to V-628. Turn right and drive west for 2½ miles to the entrance of Meredyth Vineyards. This is one of Virginia's largest commercial vineyards, with fifty-five acres of French-American and European (vinifera) vines. Wines include Aurora Blanc, de Chaunac, Seyval Blanc, Chardonnay, Riesling, Cabernet Sauvignon, Villard Blanc, and Villard Noir. Visitors are invited to tour the vineyards and see French-American vines from nursery to bearing vineyard rows, as well as Asiatic-European vinifera. Guides are most helpful in explaining the vineyard's methods and answering your questions. Tours are daily without need for appointments. Bring a lunch if you'd like, purchase a bottle of wine, and enjoy a picnic on the grounds. Groups of more than ten people should arrange for tours in advance, and a nominal group rate is charged. (540) 687-6277.

Piedmont Vineyards and Winery, Inc. From US-50 at Middleburg take V-626 south for approximately 3 miles to Halfway Road and the Piedmont Vineyards. Piedmont seems to be as proud of its thirty acres of fine vineyards as it is proud of its knowledgeable founder, Mrs. Thomas Furness. Beginning with vineyard plantings in 1973, Mrs. Furness aspired to produce the finest quality white wines. She is the only woman to date who has single-handedly started a vineyard and winery operation. Mrs. Furness was seventy-five at the time of Piedmont's inception. Acres of Chardonnay, Semillon, and Seyval Blanc are thriving with modern techniques and old-world formulas. Tours are given without charge. Fee charged for groups greater than ten people. (540) 687-5528.

LEESBURG, VA

Originally called Georgetown in honor of George II, Leesburg was chartered by the English Crown in 1757 to have seventy half-acre lots and six streets. Shortly thereafter a bill was introduced to rename Georgetown Leesburgh (now Leesburg), in honor of Francis Lightfoot Lee. Located between the Potomac River and the Blue Ridge Mountains in the rolling countryside of northern Virginia, Leesburg takes you through two centuries of American history with authentic buildings of diverse architecture. Narrow streets, brick sidewalks, quaint shops, and a variety of fine restaurants add up to an enjoyable day trip experience. Designated a Historic District by the Virginia Landmarks Commission, Leesburg has especially worthwhile walking tours. The Visitors Center, located at 108 South Street, will provide additional information at (703) 777-0519. Bring your camera or your sketch pad to capture the architecture of original, historic buildings and scenes of easy, Southern life.

WHERE TO GO

Loudoun Museum. Located at 16 Loudoun Street SW, Leesburg. A video enables visitors to experience much of the history and beauty of Loudoun's towns, villages, and countryside. Visitors are invited to examine the variety of local artifacts on display, which range from Indian arrowheads and pottery to artifacts from the battle at Ball's Bluff during the Civil War. For $1.00 visitors may purchase a handsomely illustrated walking-tour map of Leesburg. Museum admission is free. (703) 777-7427. "Retrospect," a district of shops near the museum, is highly recommended. (703) 777-8277.

Oatlands. Located approximately 6 miles south of Leesburg on US-15. You may want to tour this beautiful classic Greek Revival mansion and plantation first, while en route to Leesburg from Middleburg. Oatlands is one of seventeen historic properties of the National Trust for Historic Preservation.

Located in the heart of northern Virginia's Hunt Country, this marvelous mansion was once the center of a thriving 3,400-acre plantation. Oatlands House, constructed shortly after 1800, was partially remodeled in 1827. A front portico with hand-carved Corinthian capitals was added later. Confederate troops were billeted in the house during the Civil War. Boxwood, magnolias, and a gazebo grace the terraced formal gardens planned by Oatland's builder George Carter, a great-grandson of famed planter Robert "King" Carter. Greek Revival ornament adorns an interior filled with French and American art and antiques.

Springtime visitors to the property enjoy the Loudoun Hunt Point-to-Point races in mid-April and a foxhound show in May. Today the beauty of Oatlands and its 261 acres of farmland is protected by a series of scenic easements, which insure the estate's continuing role as a center of cultural life and equestrian sports in Loudoun County, Virginia. Open for tours daily from April to December. Fee. (703) 777-3174.

Morven Park. Located at the western end of Leesburg. Take US-7 west to Old Waterford Road and the entrance of Morven Park. Enter the 1,200 acres of this Virginia estate down a tree-lined, mile-long drive past formal boxwood gardens to the stately mansion. The mansion, focal point of the estate, evolved from a fieldstone farmhouse in 1781 to its present turn-of-the-century appearance. Enter the mansion through a Greek Revival portico to see a Renaissance great hall, a Jacobean dining room, a French drawing room, and library. Furnishings include sixteenth-century Flemish tapestries, fine paintings, and porcelain figurines.

In addition to the magnificent mansion, extensive formal gardens, and nature trails, there is a carriage museum housing more than one hundred horse-drawn vehicles. Throughout the year, equestrian events are held on the grounds. Fee. (703) 777-2414.

WATERFORD, VA

Two-and-one-half centuries of history are preserved in this tiny village clustered around a mill on the banks of the Catoctin Creek. Settled in 1733 by Quakers from Pennsylvania, the village hasn't grown since the mid-nineteenth century. Today the brick, stone, and frame buildings are still nestled quietly in the Catoctin Valley, surrounded by the fertile, rolling farmland of northwestern Virginia. In 1970, the entire village—houses, barns, shops, schools, churches, and fields— was designated a National Historic Landmark. Waterford is not a restoration, but a living village, where the past mingles with the present in an unbroken line of events. From Leesburg take V-7 west to V-665 north to Waterford. With the exception of a three-day Homes Tour and Crafts Exhibit that is held each year in early October (most properties are privately owned and occupied), village residences are not open for tours. Visits to Waterford are best planned from the perspective of a self-guided walking tour through its charming streets. The Waterford Historic Preservation Association at Main and Second Streets will provide further information. (540) 882-3018. While the commercialism of restaurants has not come to the area, local residents feel that the best place to start your visit here is at the friendly **Waterford Market on Factory Street.** Here, a country store environment offers light refreshments at a modest price and well-seasoned tourist advice for free.

POINT OF ROCKS, MD

Point of Rocks was a strategic site during the Civil War. While no major encounters took place here, there were many skirmishes and raids. It was here that General Joseph Hooker received telegraphed orders to turn over the Army of the Potomac to General Meade just before the Battle of Gettysburg.

The area received national attention in 1830 when the proponents of the B&O Railroad and the C&O Canal fought over the right-of-way on the narrow strip of land here between the base of Catoctin Mountain and the Potomac.

Today visitors enjoy the prime fishing waters here. Day trip drivers will find it to be a scenic drive at the end of this busy itinerary.

From Waterford take V-662 south to V-7 east to Leesburg, then go north on US-15 to Point of Rocks. For return routing to Baltimore at the end of this day trip, continue east on M-28 to M-85 north and pick up I-70 east (just outside of Frederick) to Baltimore.

Day Trips from Baltimore

Travel west to a route rich in cultural history. This fertile approach to the Piedmont region attracted a diverse mixture of peoples—English, Scotch, and German. Rich farmland and prolific fur trapping brought increasing numbers of settlements as the population eased itself westward toward new markets. This corridor became a mecca for ambitious young Americans approaching the gateway to the western frontier. Vital north-south and east-west trade routes were established as towns prospered.

Towns grew around grist, paper, and saw mills, which functioned as centers for trade. In the western part of the state grain and livestock were preferred over the preoccupation with tobacco in southern Maryland. Flour, whiskey, and hides were prominent exports.

Today's visitors can feel the presence of the past in Ellicott City, the charming child of Ellicott Mills. Shops filled with crafts, memorabilia, and home-baked goods are nested in original buildings of the old mill town. Samples of Americana are sold at New Market, "The Antique Capital of Maryland." Gentle grades yield to the encroaching climbs of the Piedmont region en route to the small scenic towns of Middletown and Mount Airy.

Follow the path of the Civil War to Antietam where the scene is virtually unchanged since the battle. For more Civil War history, visit Harpers Ferry, site of John Brown's notorious raid.

Smooth, uninterrupted driving on I-70 west will deliver you easily to our day trips, but you may welcome the opportunity to drive along the back roads into the history of western Maryland and West Virginia.

ELLICOTT CITY, MD

Three Quaker brothers founded this town in about 1772 on the Patapsco River and made it one of the greatest milling and manufacturing towns in the East during its heyday. Later, the town became the location of an ironworks and, most important, the first terminus for the B&O Railroad.

While the town's adjacency to the river was a boon to local industry, flooding over the years has destroyed many of the town's historic buildings. Those that remain include the stone buildings along **Tongue Row,** which now house specialty shops; the **Colonial Inn and Opera House,** which is reported to be the site where John Wilkes Booth made his acting debut; **Disney's Tavern** (1790); **Mount Ida** (1828), the last home built by an Ellicott; and the former **Patapsco Hotel,** a popular lodging facility during the development of the B&O Railroad.

From Baltimore, take US–40 west to Rogers Avenue southeast (M–99) for 1 mile to Old Frederick Road. Turn left on Old Frederick Road, which becomes Main Street in Ellicott City.

WHERE TO GO

Ellicott City B&O Railroad Station Museum. Maryland Avenue and Main Street. Begin your visit at this 1831 building, which was the first terminus of the first railroad in the United States. Today the station serves as a museum of railroad memorabilia and an information center where visitors can see a sight-and-sound show and a

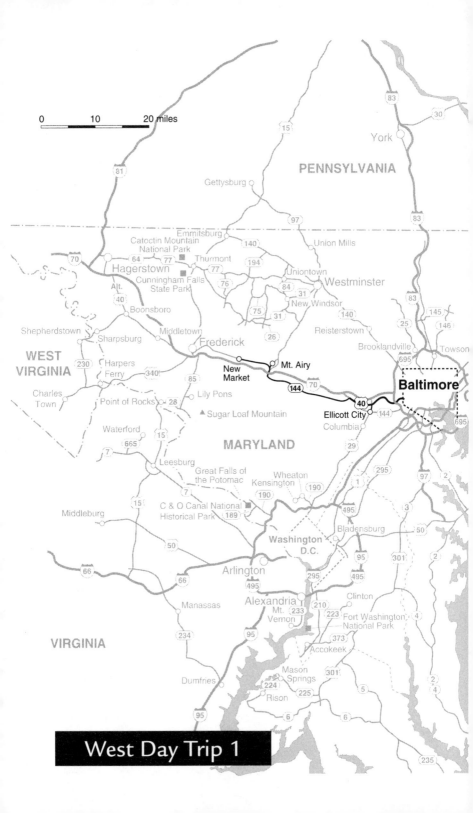

West Day Trip 1

working model train display and browse in a gift shop. Fee. Call (410) 461-1944.

Tongue Row. This quaint street in midtown, just off Main Street, is lined with original stone homes. Today it is the site of interesting specialty shops and seasonal crafts exhibits.

Walking Tour. A brochure describes a self-guided walking tour of the city's historic district. It is distributed by many area merchants. Free.

WHERE TO EAT

Cacao Lane Restaurant. Located at 8066 Main Street. This popular restaurant located in the heart of the historic district features consistently good food, served attractively, in a friendly atmosphere. Cuisine is American and Continental. It is open seven days a week, year-round. The manager recommends reservations for parties of more than four persons. Lunch, $; dinner, $$; ☐. (410) 461-1378.

MOUNT AIRY, MD

Located in the rich, fertile tracts of land in Frederick County's wine region, Mount Airy is a tiny rural town with a traditional Main Street. To get there from Ellicott City, return to Old Frederick Road via Main Street, take a short shunt on US-40 west, and pick up M-144 west (Frederick Road) for a scenic approach. For a more time-efficient route, remain on US-40 west until it runs concurrent with I-70 west. Continue on this route to Mount Airy's Main Street. Turn right and drive northbound into the town.

WHERE TO GO

Berrywine Plantations. Located at 13601 Glisans Mill Road. From Main Street drive west on Prospect Road and continue on to Jacobs Road. Turn right on Woodville Road, and drive north to Glisans Mill Road. This 230-acre plantation is a family-run business founded in 1971. The first plantings of French hybrid grapes were begun in 1972. Today Berrywine features French and Italian styles of red and rosé wines, as well as German-style white wines. In addition, semisweet table and dessert wines are available. Besides the fine wines, the plantation offers a magnificent view of Catoctin Mountain toward Camp David in Thurmont.

There is a gift shop on the premises, and picnic facilities are available. Guided tours available. Free. (410) 795-6432.

If time allows and you'd like to visit two additional vineyards, you might include Elk Run Vineyards, 11513 Liberty Road, Mt. Airy, (410) 775-2513, and Loew Vineyards, a neighbor at 14001 Liberty Road, (301) 831-5464. Both offer tours and tastings.

NEW MARKET, MD

The **Historic District of New Market** is a fine example of a small town of the late Federal period. In New Market, dubbed "The Antique Capital of Maryland," the tree-shaded main street and a few of the side streets boast more than forty antiques, crafts, and specialty shops. Merchants offer everything from candles and dollhouse furniture to country crafts and period antiques. All shops are open year-round. For tours and information, call (301) 865-3318.

Continue west on US-40 from Mount Airy to New Market at the junction of M-75.

New Market Days is an annual celebration scheduled in late September. It includes good country food, buggy rides, historical displays, and entertainment. Free. For more information about this specific event, write to Mr. Frank Shaw, c/o New Market, Maryland 21774. (See Festivals and Celebrations listing at back of book.)

For return routing to Baltimore, drive east on M-144 to US-40 east near Ellicott City, and follow this road to Baltimore. If you have time, you might want to continue northwest on M-144 and pick up I-70/US-40 west into Frederick for the first stop in Day Trip 2 of this section.

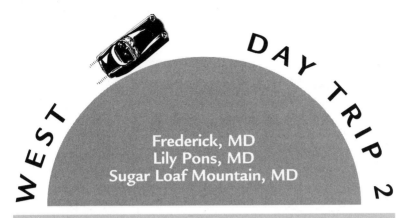

FREDERICK, MD

Founded in 1745 by English and German settlers, this delightful town was originally called Fredericktown. As a frontier town it served the wagon trains that traveled through the surrounding fertile farmland on their way west across the mountains. Frederick has a wealth of historic points. From Baltimore take US–40 west to I-70/US–40 directly to Frederick. Get off at the Patrick Street exit and follow signs to the visitor center.

WHERE TO GO

Visitor Center. Located at 19 East Church Street. Information regarding the guided, one-and-a-half-hour walking tours on weekends and holidays from April to December originating at the Visitor Center is available here. Fee for tours. Children under twelve, free. General visitor information is also available. Free. (301) 663–8687 or (800) 999–3613. Carriage tours are available, (301) 694–7433.

Barbara Fritchie House. Located at 154 West Patrick Street. This is a reconstruction of the home of the ardent Unionist Barbara Fritchie. The story is told that the ninety-five-year-old patriot dauntlessly waved her Union flag as Stonewall Jackson and his troops marched through town in 1862. According to the classic Civil War poem by John Greenleaf Whittier, she challenged him not to harm a hair on her old gray head!

Today the home rests on its original site and contains articles of historical interest. Fee. Discounts to children under twelve and, of

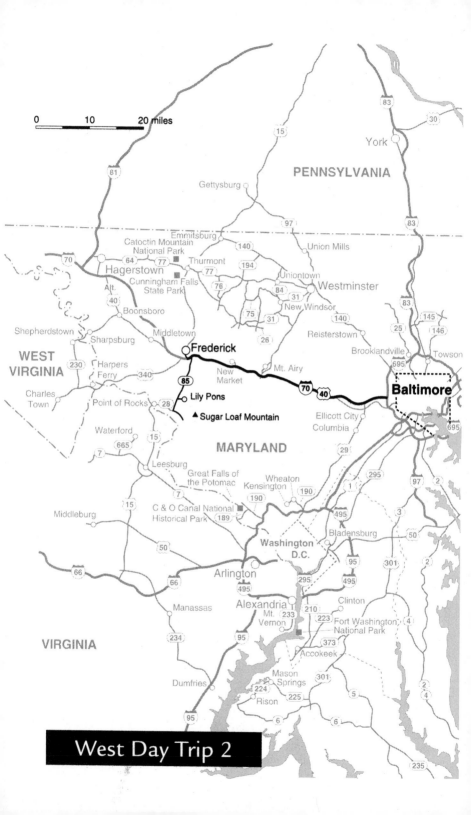

0   10   20 miles

PENNSYLVANIA

York

Gettysburg

15

97

83

83

30

Emmitsburg
Catoctin Mountain
National Park
Thurmont
140
Union Mills

81

70

64   77

Hagerstown

Cunningham Falls
State Park

Alt.
40

Boonsboro

194

77

76

Uniontown

Westminster

84   31

New Windsor

31

140

Reisterstown

83

25

145

146

Shepherdstown

Sharpsburg

Middletown

Frederick

75

26

Mt. Airy

Brooklandville

Towson

WEST
VIRGINIA

230

Harpers
Ferry

340

New
Market

85

695

Baltimore

Charles
Town

Point of Rocks

28

Lily Pons

▲ Sugar Loaf Mountain

70   40

Ellicott City
Columbia

695

Waterford

665

7

15

MARYLAND

29

Leesburg

Great Falls of
the Potomac

Wheaton
Kensington

190

295

97

2

Middleburg

15

7

C & O Canal National
Historical Park

189

190

495

1

3

50

Bladensburg

50

66

66

Arlington

495

Washington
D.C.

295

95

301

495

2

Manassas

Alexandria

Mt.   233
Vernon

210

223

Clinton

Fort Washington
National Park

4

234

95

373

Accokeek

VIRGINIA

Dumfries

Mason
Springs

224

301

225

Rison

5

2
4

6

6

235

95

West Day Trip 2

course, senior citizens older than sixty (Barbara would have liked it that way). (301) 698–0630.

Schifferstadt. Located at 1110 Rosemont Avenue. Constructed about 1756, this structure is a fine example of the cultural heritage of this town and of early building methods. Exhibits of arts and crafts are on display here. Fee. (301) 663–6225.

Mount Olivet Cemetery. Located at the end of Market Street, this cemetery is the final resting place of such noted Americans as Francis Scott Key and his wife, as well as Barbara Fritchie and more than 400 Confederate soldiers from the battles of Antietam and Monocacy. Also buried here is Thomas Johnson, Maryland's first governor. Open to the public. Call (301) 662–1164.

Rose Hill Manor Children's Museum. Located at 1661 North Market Street. Originally the home of Maryland's first governor, Thomas Johnson, the house (1790), carriages, and garden are restored to show nineteenth-century family life. Hands-on displays delight the children, and guide service is available. Fee. (301) 694–1648.

The National Museum of Civil War Medicine. Located at 48 East Patrick Street, Frederick. The only museum in the world devoted exclusively to telling the medical story of the Civil War; the aftermath of the battle, the care and comfort of the wounded, the caregivers, and the innovations in medicine during the period. Features rare artifacts, including an ambulance wagon, surgeon's tent, traveling medical chests, stretchers, medical and dental instruments, a holding coffin, and a realistic amputation video (not for the squeamish!). Museum store, group tours, and Kids' Corner. Living history demonstrations are scheduled periodically. Fee. (301) 695–1864.

WHERE TO EAT

Red Horse Steak House. Located at the junction of US–40 and US–15 in Frederick, this restaurant's apple-red horse atop the building is a local landmark. The Red Horse specializes in steaks, fresh seafood, and prime rib. Dinner is served seven days a week; lunch is served five days a week. Breakfast is served in the Coffee Shop in the adjoining motel. $$; ☐. (301) 663–3030.

di Francesco's. Located at 26 North Market Street. A pleasant Italian restaurant featuring homemade pastas, sauces, and breads. Children's menu. Reservations suggested. $$; ☐. (301) 695–5499.

LILY PONS, MD

Located in the beautiful countryside of Frederick County, this destination is for the nature lover and curiosity seeker alike. Leave Frederick on M-355 south. Pass over I-70 to M-85 south, which is Buckeystown Pike. After passing Buckeystown, drive 3 miles to Lily Pons Road. Turn left and drive east across the Monocacy River to the fish hatchery and water gardens.

Lilypons Water Gardens. Lily Pons Road, Lily Pons. This site is one of the largest suppliers of ornamental fish and aquatic plants in the world. Lilies are in bloom from late May through August. The water garden is named after Metropolitan Opera star Lily Pons, who visited the site. Free. (301) 874-5133.

SUGAR LOAF MOUNTAIN, MD

This mountain is within 3,000 acres of privately owned countryside known as Stronghold. The estate was deeded to the Stronghold Corporation by its owner, Gordon Strong, to provide a natural preserve for the public to enjoy. More than 100,000 visitors come to Stronghold each year.

From Lilypons Water Gardens, continue east on Lily Pons Road to Park Mills Road. Turn left and drive northeast to Mount Ephraim Road. Turn right and drive southeast to Comus Road, which is within the Sugar Loaf Mountain Natural Area.

WHERE TO GO

Sugar Loaf Mountain. Early settlers gave the mountain its name because its shape reminded them of this household staple. Sugar Loaf rises 1,281 feet above the surrounding countryside. Lookouts were placed on its slopes during the Civil War. Today visitors may stop at several lookout points carved into the natural surroundings to view the farmland of Montgomery County, the Potomac River and Frederick valleys, and the Catoctin and Blue Ridge mountains.

Hiking and picnicking are the favored activities here. Free.

Return routing to Baltimore through lovely Frederick County, at the end of this day trip, offers glimpses of valley vistas, seasonal foliage, and country communities. Return to Park Mills Road and turn right. Continue to drive northwest until you reach Fingerboard Road (M-80). Turn right and drive east, toward Urbana, and follow this route to Fountain Mills. Turn left and drive north on M-75 to New Market. Stop here for refreshment, or continue on to Baltimore via M-144 east or I-70/US-40 east.

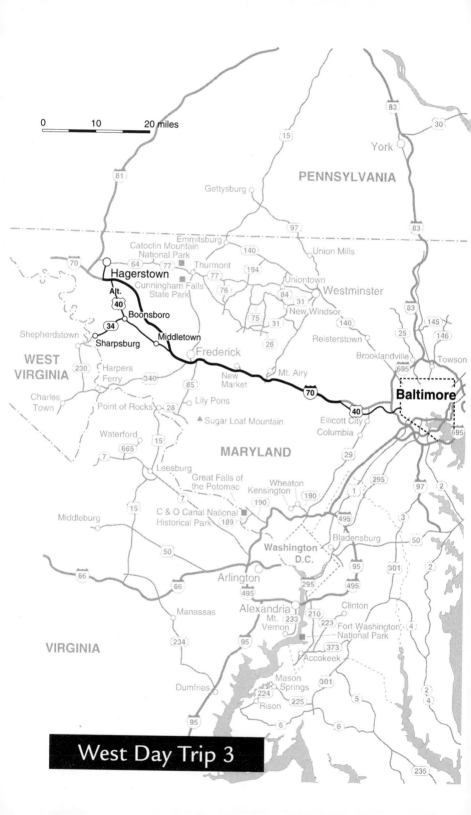

West Day Trip 3

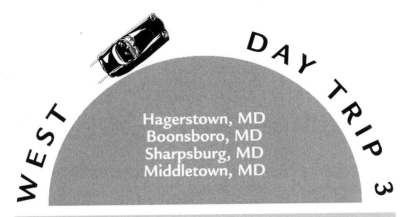

Hagerstown, MD
Boonsboro, MD
Sharpsburg, MD
Middletown, MD

HAGERSTOWN, MD

Settlers first came to this area as a part of the movement west. In 1739, a German immigrant named Jonathan Hager settled here with his wife, Elizabeth. He called this site Hager's Delight and went on to found Elizabethtown in 1762. Later on, the two sites were officially established as Hagerstown. Today many of the existing structures are reminders of the life and times of the eighteenth and nineteenth centuries.

Although the destinations in this day trip are relatively far from Baltimore, time-efficient routing will get you there fast. From Baltimore, take US-40 west to I-70 west to exit 32 northwest into Hagerstown. From the exit 32 cloverleaf, the main thoroughfare into town is US-40 west.

WHERE TO GO

Hagerstown City Park. Virginia Avenue. Rated the second most beautiful natural city park in the nation, this spot is a welcoming oasis to visitors. It features quiet picnic areas, beautiful flowered and wooded park areas, and a lake graced by majestic swans. Free.

Washington County Museum of Fine Arts. Located within the Hagerstown City Park, this stately Georgian brick museum overlooks the park lake. It houses a permanent collection of fine arts that showcases the American School. Free; donations accepted. (301) 739-5727.

Hager House and Museum. Key Street, City Park. Built in 1739 by the town founder, Jonathan Hager, this stone residence is unique.

It was constructed over a spring, so that during an Indian attack the family would not be cut off from their water supply. The museum includes eighteenth-century artifacts excavated on the site. Fee. (301) 739-8393.

Miller House Museum and the Valley Store Museum. Located at 135 West Washington Street. The Washington County Historical Society Headquarters and an information center are located in this Federal period home. Special exhibits are featured each month and include an extensive collection of dolls, antique clocks, C&O Canal memorabilia, and Civil War artifacts.

The Valley Store Museum, in the basement, is a reconstruction of a country store, complete with merchandise authentic to the years spanning 1840 to 1918. Fee. (301) 797-8782.

WHERE TO EAT

Tortuga Restaurant. 901 Dual Highway (US-40). Serving breakfast, lunch, and dinner. International American. $-$$; □. (301) 739-2707.

Richardson's Restaurant. 710 Dual Highway (US-40). Open for breakfast, lunch, and dinner, this traditional restaurant bakes its own bread to accompany its steaks and seafood. $-$$; □. (301) 733-3660.

BOONSBORO, MD

Settled in 1774 by George and William Boone, who were said to have been related to the more famous Daniel, this town prospered in the 1830s when the National Pike was alive with westward moving traffic. During the Civil War, battles were fought in nearby areas by such famous Americans as Stonewall Jackson and J.E.B. Stuart.

From Frederick Street in Hagerstown, drive south onto the Old National Pike. This is also designated Alternate US-40. This route traverses farmlands and scenic valleys with vistas of Catoctin and South mountains as it brings you directly into Boonsboro.

WHERE TO GO

Doug Bast's Boonsborough Museum of History. Located at 113 North Main Street. Exhibits include Civil War relics, historical weapons, Indian artifacts, and early Boonsborough memorabilia. Mr. Bast began assembling his collection as a child in the community. It is a never-ending project of love and well worth a visit when in the area. Fee. (301) 432-6969.

Crystal Grottoes Caverns. Exit Boonsboro, southwest, on M-34 for 1 mile to the caverns. Underground limestone wonders are the result of millions of years of chemical and mineral action. Born of nature and sculpted by man, these corridors of stalagmites and stalactites depict mythological and modern beings. Guided tours available. Fee. (301) 432-6336.

Washington Monument State Park. Return to Boonsboro and drive south for a short distance on Alternate US-40 to the Washington Monument State Park. Besides general natural beauty, the main attraction in this park is the Washington Monument. It was erected in one day by the citizens of Boonsboro on July 4, 1827, and was the first monument built to the memory of George Washington. For hardier visitors, the monument can be reached by walking ¼ mile uphill from the ample parking lot. Free. (301) 791-4767.

WHERE TO EAT

Schmankerl Stube. Located at 58 South Potomac Street, Hagerstown. Host Charlie Pekula, a native Bavarian, brought some of his region's finest cuisine to the heart of Maryland's German community. But, it's enjoyed by anyone who loves authentic Bavarian dining. There are lots of fun festivities here throughout the year. $$; ☐. (301) 797-3354.

Old South Mountain Inn. Located on Alternate US-40 across from the entrance to Washington Monument State Park, this historic stone inn dates back to 1730. Early American atmosphere and reliably well-prepared meals are featured. Children's menu available. $$; ☐. (301) 432-6155.

SHARPSBURG, MD

The Battle of Antietam (or Sharpsburg) on September 17, 1862, climaxed the first of Confederate General Robert E. Lee's two attempts to carry the war into the North. Some 41,000 Southerners were pitted against the 87,000-man Federal Army of the Potomac under

General George B. McClellan. When the fighting ended, the course of the Civil War had been greatly altered.

More men were killed or wounded here on that infamous date in 1862 than on any other single day of the Civil War. Federal losses were 12,410; Confederate losses were 10,700. Although neither side gained a decisive victory, Lee's failure to carry the war effort effectively into the North caused Great Britain to postpone recognition of the Confederate government. The battle also gave President Abraham Lincoln the opportunity to issue the Emancipation Proclamation, which, on January 1, 1863, declared that all slaves in states still in rebellion against the United States would be free. Henceforth the war had a dual purpose: to preserve the Union and to end slavery.

From Alternate US–40, just south of Boonsboro, take M–34 southwest (Shepherdstown Pike) through Keedysville to Sharpsburg.

WHERE TO GO

Antietam National Battlefield. From M–34 (Main Street) in Sharpsburg, travel east to M–65 (Hagerstown Pike). Turn left and drive north to the entrance of the battlefield. The Battle of Antietam was fought over an area of 12 square miles and consisted of three basic phases: morning, midday, and afternoon. Before touring the battlefield, go to the visitors center where exhibits and an eighteen-minute slide program provide an introduction to the Maryland campaign. Especially impressive is the panoramic view of the battlefield, complete with explanation of battle strategies. Information regarding driving tours is available here. Free.

Other stops along the tour include **Bloody Lane,** the site where the greatest number of fatalities occurred, and **Burnside Bridge,** named for the Union general whose troops attempted to cross the bridge during the battle. The **Dunkard Church** (c. 1852) was used as a makeshift fort by the Confederate army and was badly riddled by shot and shell from the Federal forces. It was rebuilt in 1863.

The battlefield is on the National Register of Historic Places. The park has a picnic area. Fishing is permitted in Antietam Creek; a Maryland fishing license is required. Relic hunting within the park is prohibited. Free. (301) 432–5124.

C&O Canal National Historic Park Headquarters. Located a short distance west of Sharpsburg on M–34, just before the James

Rumsey Bridge. The park administrative offices and an informed, helpful staff offer brochures on area attractions and specific information regarding the C&O Canal. Free. (301) 793-4200.

Ranger Station. Canal Road. The station is located in the immediate area of the park headquarters. Convenient free parking gives the inquiring visitor ample time to pick up maps of the C&O Canal and general park information. Take advantage of the towpath access here to enjoy a stroll along the historic canal. Free. (301) 739-6179.

From Sharpsburg, return via M-34 east to Alternate US-40 south. Turn right onto the Old National Pike in Middletown.

MIDDLETOWN, MD

Middletown is an immaculately clean community with charming Americana houses. It has an air of old-fashioned comfort and homestead pride.

Several Civil War skirmishes in the vicinity crowded Middletown homes and churches with wounded soldiers. Young Nancy Crouse, an early Middletown resident, is said to have wrapped the Union flag around her when the Confederate troops galloped into town. Unfortunately, Southern gallantry was at an all-time low point, and the flag was torn from her body and destroyed.

Settled in the eighteenth century by people of English and German descent, the town was incorporated in 1833. Today visitors pause to appreciate this picture-postcard town. For day trip drivers, it marks a pleasant conclusion to a busy day.

When departing Middletown for return routing to Baltimore, continue southeast on Alternate US-40 into Frederick. Here, you can take M-144 east to US-40 east, or take I-70/US-40 east into Baltimore.

If you choose to extend your day trip while still in Sharpsburg, continue southwest on M-34 into Shepherdstown, the first destination in Day Trip 4 of this chapter.

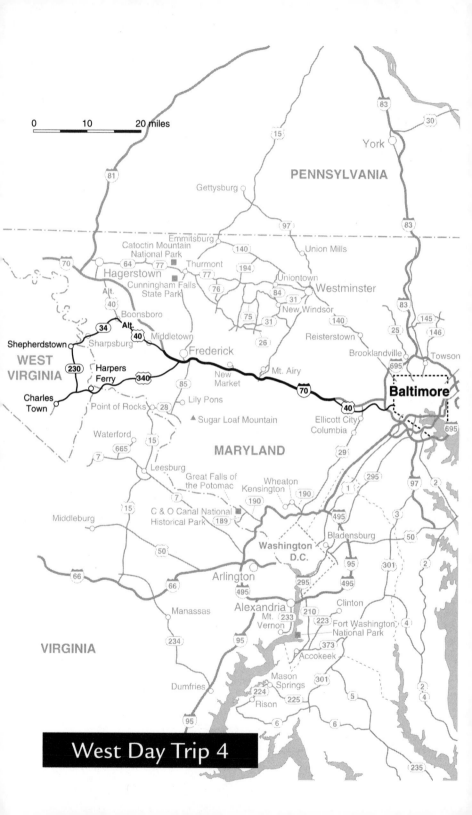

West Day Trip 4

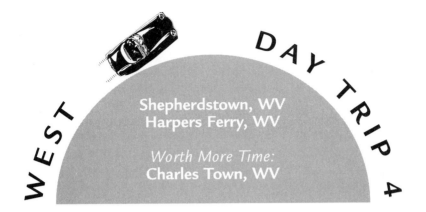

WEST

DAY TRIP 4

Shepherdstown, WV
Harpers Ferry, WV

Worth More Time:
Charles Town, WV

SHEPHERDSTOWN, WV

Shepherdstown was chartered in 1764, and early settlers reached it by traveling south from York to Lancaster, Pennsylvania, on the Old Philadelphia Wagon Road. Most of these early settlers were of German descent, with a sprinkling of English, Scottish, and Dutch families.

Among their ranks were potters, smiths, and other craftsmen, as well as merchants and industrialists who gave the town an economic base. One such entrepreneur was James Rumsey, who invented and successfully demonstrated the operation of his steam-powered boat on the Potomac River here on December 3, 1787. The town flourished during the eighteenth and nineteenth centuries with the Town Run providing the power to turn the wheels of its industry.

Because of its strategic location, 4 miles south of Antietam Battlefield and 10 miles west of Harpers Ferry, Shepherdstown saw much activity during the Civil War. At the time of the Battle of Antietam, the town became a huge field hospital sheltering wounded Confederate soldiers.

Shepherdstown also played an important part in the history of the C&O Canal. Directly across the Potomac River from Canal Lock #38 are the remains of the dock and warehouse area of the town. From there, Canal barges loaded with farm products were poled across the river to enter the canal through the Shepherdstown Lock and continued to markets in Georgetown and Alexandria, Virginia.

Today visitors enjoy driving through this quiet, country town to sense the presence of its history, especially in the downtown area, which has been designated a historical district on the National Register.

From Baltimore, take US–40 west to I–70 west. Then take exit 49 off I–70, just outside Frederick. From here, pick up Alternate US–40 west (south of Boonsboro). Then follow M–34 west across the Potomac River to nearby Shepherdstown.

WHERE TO GO

Entler Hotel. Located on Main Street, which can be reached by WV–230. This hotel opened in 1786. In the early 1970s, it was restored by the Historic Shepherdstown Commission. Today this hotel is the home of the Historic Shepherdstown Museum, which displays furnishings that enable visitors to see how life was lived in Shepherdstown in the eighteenth century. Free. (304) 876–0910.

James Rumsey Monument. At the north end of Mill Street stands the commemorative obelisk dedicated to the industrial genius of James Rumsey, who gave the first public demonstration of the steamboat in 1787.

Shepherd Grist Mill. Mill and High Streets, Shepherdstown. The mill was constructed in 1739 by Thomas Shepherd, founder of Shepherdstown. With a diameter of 40 feet, the overshot waterwheel is said to be one of the world's largest. Today it is privately owned. While it is not open for tours, take the opportunity while shopping in the High Street district to walk by it.

O'Hurley's General Store. Located at 205 East Washington Street (WV–230). This sprawling country store sells homestead supplies such as sleds, glassware, dry goods, cast-iron cookware, and crockery. A colorful brochure lists more of their inventory: enamelware, fruit presses, baskets, and dinner bells. If this colorful combination intrigues you, you might want to accept the following invitation from this family-run establishment: "Homesteaders, housewives and others wishing our circular will be furnished same by sending us their addresses." A replica of James Rumsey's steam-powered boat is also on display here. (304) 876–6907.

WHERE TO EAT

Bavarian Inn and Lodge. From Shepherdstown, this property is 1 mile north on WV–480 at the west end of the Potomac River Bridge. The award-winning Bavarian Inn and lodge is West Virginia's top-rated country inn and restaurant. Beautiful guest rooms, some with fireplaces, overlook the Potomac River. The restaurant features fine German cuisine and serves breakfast, lunch, and dinner. Wild game and other specialties are served in season. Children's menu is available. Reservations are advised. $$-$$$; ☐. (304) 876-2551.

Yellow Brick Bank Restaurant. German and Princess Streets, Shepherdstown. A corner bank was transformed into this colorful restaurant, which features an excellent, varied menu served in a charming atmosphere that is sure to please. An excellent Sunday brunch is served. Reservations are recommended. $$; ☐. (304) 876-2208.

Gary's Zittle's Old Sweet Shoppe. Located at 100 West German Street. This little gem features some of the finest baked goods and pastries this side of the Alps. It also offers whole grain and cholesterol free European breads. On a cold day, it's a great place for hot chocolate or coffee and a calorie or two. Call (800) 9-BAKERY.

HARPERS FERRY, WV

Harpers Ferry, situated on a point of land at the confluence of the Shenandoah and Potomac rivers and dominated by the Blue Ridge Mountains, was a beckoning wilderness in the early 1700s. By the mid-nineteenth century, it was a town of some 3,000 inhabitants, an important arms-producing center, and a transportation link between east and west. John Brown's raid in 1859 and the Civil War thrust the town into national prominence. The destruction wrought by the war and repeated flooding were responsible for the town's eventual decline.

The first settler on this land was Peter Stephens, a trader, who came here in 1733 and set up a primitive ferry service at the junction of the two rivers. Fourteen years later, Robert Harper, a millwright and the man for whom the town is named, settled here, taking over Stephens' ferry operation. Seeing the waterpower potential, he later built a mill. The ferry and the mill have long since disappeared.

Within a century, Harpers Ferry developed from a tiny village into an industrialized community. Then came disaster. In October 1859, John Brown's abolitionist raid jarred the peaceful town. The Civil War that followed seventeen months later left a path of destruction that wrecked the town's economy. The armory and arsenal buildings were burned in 1861 to keep them from falling into Confederate hands. Because of the town's location and its railway system, Union and Confederate troops frequently moved through Harpers Ferry, and soldiers of both armies occupied the town intermittently throughout the war.

The largest military operation against Harpers Ferry occurred prior to the Battle of Antietam in September 1862 when Confederate forces under General Stonewall Jackson seized the town and captured the 12,700-man Union garrison commanded by Colonel Dixon Miles.

Discouraged by continual war damage and the lack of employment, many townspeople moved away. For years afterward, empty buildings stood in silent desolation, and once-active industrial sites were slowly reclaimed by nature.

The one bright hope in the story of Harpers Ferry after the Civil War was the establishment of a normal school for the education of freed blacks. The first classroom of what was to become Storer College was located in the Lockwood House, an abandoned armory dwelling above the town. The college remained in operation until 1955.

Today Harpers Ferry stands as a living museum describing the actions of a man whose words and deeds prophesied the advent of the Civil War.

Harpers Ferry National Historic Park is a remarkable restoration of a time and events in America's history. It offers twenty-three points of interest within and around the area. The park entrance is located on US–340 at Shenandoah Street.

WHERE TO GO

Visitors Center. Located on Shenandoah Street near High Street. Begin your visit to the park with an introductory video program and exhibits on the park themes. Information on self-guided and conducted walking tours is also available here. Most of the theme activities in the park are during the summer months, when costumed guides explain the significance of points of interest.

The **Jefferson County Visitor Bureau/West Virginia Welcome Center** at the corner of US–340 and Washington Street provides complete tourist information on all of Jefferson County and on the entire state of West Virginia. For information before arriving, write Jefferson County Visitors Bureau, P.O. Box A, Harpers Ferry, WV 25425, or call (800) 848-8687 or (304) 535-2627.

In the fall and spring, park activities are restricted to weekends, but the center and some historic buildings remain open. Picnicking and camping are permitted in the immediate area. Call the visitors center for details. For information, write the Park Superintendent, Box 65, Harpers Ferry, WV 24525. Open all year, except Christmas and New Year's Day. Free. (304) 535-6223.

A word about John Brown. John Brown, 1800-1859, was the man whose raid brought Harpers Ferry to national attention. An ardent abolitionist, he fixed upon Harpers Ferry as the starting point for the insurrection against slavery. Brown and his twenty-two-man "army of liberation" attacked the town on the night of October 16, 1859, seizing the armory and several other strategic points. They were captured, brought to trial for murder and treason, and hanged on December 2, 1859. On the day of his execution, Brown prophesied that the crimes of society could only be purged by bloodshed. Sixteen months later, on April 12, 1861, the war that John Brown seemed to foretell began at a place called Fort Sumter in Charleston Harbor, South Carolina.

HARPERS FERRY TOUR

Begin your tour of Harpers Ferry at High Street, located 1 block past the visitors center. This becomes the main street of the historic district. Many sites and shops located on High Street are ones that you will want to visit. No numerical designations assign addresses to these sites, but you'll easily find them as you walk, beginning at Shenandoah Street, along High Street. As High Street leaves the immediate historic district, it becomes Washington Street. Thus, sites indicated on Washington Street are actually located on an extension of High Street. The town is small. Patience and a good pair of comfortable shoes will take you wherever you might want to go.

HISTORIC SITES

Primarily relating to the events surrounding John Brown's raid and the Civil War that followed, sites include: the **Harper House** (c.

1755), the oldest structure in the park; **Arsenal Square,** the foundations of the two U.S. Arsenal buildings that were burned when Federal troops evacuated the town at the beginning of the Civil War; **John Brown's Fort,** the Armory firehouse used as a refuge by the famous abolitionist; the **John Brown Museum,** a restored building that houses a theater and museum relating the events of the famous raid; and the **Civil War Museum,** where exhibits tell the story of the effects of the war on Harpers Ferry and its citizens.

OTHER ATTRACTIONS

John Brown Wax Museum. High Street, Harpers Ferry. This attraction provides a colorful, life-size exhibit of the story of John Brown's famous raid. Fee. (304) 535-6342.

Blue Ridge Outfitters. Located 4 miles southwest of Harpers Ferry on US-340. Half-day raft trips on the Potomac River begin just below Great Falls, where visitors paddle through spectacular Mather Gorge, a narrow, mile-long canyon with sheer 40-to-60-foot rock walls and continuous rolling waves. A picnic lunch is scheduled on an island midriver. Blue Ridge Outfitters says this is an ideal trip for beginners and veteran rafters alike through one of the most beautiful recreation areas of the East.

Trips are limited to ages ten through sixty. Fee. Reservations are required. Write to Blue Ridge Outfitters, P.O. Box 456, Harpers Ferry, WV 25425. Or call (304) 725-3444.

River and Trail Outfitters. Located at 604 Valley Road, Knoxville, MD 21758. Take US-40 north back toward Maryland and turn left onto Valley Road. Try white-water rafting or canoeing on the Shenandoah and North Branch of the Potomac River. There is also tubing on Antietam Creek, giving visitors the chance to be refreshed by this spring-fed stream. Cross-country skiing packages are available during winter months. (301) 695-5177.

For a complete listing of the white-water opportunities in the region, call (800) 879-7483.

WHERE TO EAT

Mountain House Cafe. High Street, Harpers Ferry; located in the fifteenth property west of Shenandoah Street. This sidewalk cafe, in a beautiful setting, features home-cooked, country-style food and light fare salads and sandwiches. $; ☐. (304) 535-2339.

Hilltop House. Ridge Street, Harpers Ferry. Drive west on High Street until it becomes Washington Street. At the intersection of Columbia and Washington Streets, turn right. Drive to Ridge Street and turn right again. Follow Ridge Street to its dead end in a cul-de-sac at the Hilltop House.

Once the retreat of President Woodrow Wilson, Mark Twain, and Doctor Alexander Graham Bell, the restored Hilltop House overlooks the junction of the Potomac and Shenandoah rivers and three states. Both dining and lodging are afforded here. Specialties include Southern fried chicken, baked ham, stuffed flounder, and an all-day buffet on weekends. $$; ☐. (304) 535-6321.

Cliffside Inn. US-340, Harpers Ferry. Enjoy fine American dining at breakfast, lunch, and dinner. Visitors may choose to eat buffet-style (weekends only) or to order from a menu. $; ☐. (304) 535-6302.

The Anvil. Located at 1270 Washington Street, Harpers Ferry. Enjoy dining in this quaint, rustic atmosphere. Specializing in seafood, this restaurant also offers steak, chicken, and veal. There is an "All you can eat" shrimp night on Tuesdays from 6:00 to 9:00 P.M. $-$$; ☐. (304) 535-2582.

WHERE TO SHOP

Sleepy Hollow Creations. High Street; four properties west of Shenandoah Street. West Virginia crafts, including unique candleholders, planters, and lamps sculpted from tin cans and other metals, are on sale here. A free catalog is available by mailing your request to P.O. Box 247, Harpers Ferry, WV 25425. (304) 535-2202.

Sky Mountain Jewelry Company. High Street; twelve properties west from Shenandoah Street. This is an unusual jewelry manufacturing and outlet store. Its principal products are sterling silver and gold-filled jewelry, as well as semiprecious and precious stones. Custom work, cut stones, jewelry parts, pewter, and West Virginia coal carvings are available. (304) 535-2426.

Westwind Potters. High Street; thirteenth property west from Shenandoah Street. Fine handcrafted porcelain and stoneware objects for daily use are among the fascinating display of goods here.

Expert potters have created vases, mugs, bowls, pitchers, honey pots, and other enjoyable and functional items. All wares are lead-free, as well as oven, dishwasher, and microwave safe. Commissions and mail orders are accepted by writing to P.O. Box 686, Harpers Ferry, WV 25425. (304) 535-2511.

The Harpers Ferry Flea Market is an experience. There are lots of tables filled with tools, bottles, clothes, eight-track cassettes, cooking utensils, some genuine antiques, old car parts, fruits and vegetables in season, toys, videotapes—you name it. Weekends usually from April through November. Route 340 at Bloomery Road, 1 mile south of Harpers Ferry.

WORTH MORE TIME

CHARLES TOWN, WV

Charles Town and the **Charles Town Races** are located in the Shenandoah Valley, just 6 miles west of Harpers Ferry on WV-340 in the eastern panhandle of West Virginia. Driving time is just outside our two-hour perimeter, but you may want to gather a group of friends to enjoy a day of thoroughbred racing at this beautiful track. Top off your day with convenient dining at the Skyline Terrace for a spectacular view from the terraced tables. Expenses for the day will include admission to the track and parking. Call (304) 725-7001 or (800) 795-7001.

WHERE TO GO

My Father's Workshop. Located at 1163 Washington Street. This shop features antiques, handmade Appalachian crafts, and resident woodworkers. Call before you go. P.O. Box 728, Bolivar/Harpers Ferry, WV 25425. (304) 535-2549.

Blue Ridge Outlet Center. Located at 315 West Stephen Street, Martinsburg, WV, 25401. Take WV-9 west to Queen Street, then turn right on Stephen Street. This outlet center, located in a historic woolen mill, features more than fifty quality name brand manufacturers at discount prices. Call (800) 445-3993.

Wildflower Tours. A diversity of guided tours are professionally prepared with the individual or group in mind on subjects such as history, nature, and architecture. Contact Dotty Brown to make an appointment: Dotty Brown, Tourguide, KFA Box 602, Harpers Ferry, WV 26425. (304) 725-4384.

National Fisheries Research Center. Located in Leetown, WV. Take WV-9 west, then turn left onto Leetown Pike, US-15. The visitor center features films on their research programs; live fish are also on display. Open from mid-April through October. Call (304) 876-1600.

Day Trips from Baltimore

Travel northwest to stately mansions, picturesque farmhouses, and the birthplace of Francis Scott Key. Explore 200 years of town and farm life while revisiting the Revolutionary and Civil War eras. Picture yourself in a Currier and Ives setting replete with indigenous brick-end barns.

The farmland in the northwest corridor is perhaps the most fertile in Maryland. Corn, wheat, barley, and hay fields stretch for miles over the gently rolling hills. Rich farmlands, coupled with agribusiness, set the scene for past and present lifestyles. The Carroll County Farm Museum together with the Union Mills Homestead and Grist Mill are living museums touting the central significance of the farm, its fields, and the mills. Family life was sustained by these rich tracts of land. And, for some, it was ended at Gettysburg, site of one of the most decisive battles of American history. Civil War buffs come from all over the world to visit this battlefield shrine.

Amid the natural beauty and historic treasures of Catoctin Mountain lies Thurmont, home of Camp David, the mountain retreat of America's presidents. A swing through Emmitsburg takes you to the home of the first American-born saint, Elizabeth Ann Seton, as we reach the two-hour perimeter of the northwest tours.

REISTERSTOWN, MD

Begin this day trip to the northwest corridor in Reisterstown. Although little has been preserved of its Revolutionary era, the town retains some original buildings on Main Street. Today these structures house specialty and antiques shops. From Baltimore, drive northwest on M–140 (Reisterstown Road) to reach this quaint destination.

Reisterstown was founded on a tract of land called "Reister's Desire" in 1758 by a German immigrant and innkeeper, John Reister. Just north of Reister's inn and blacksmith shop, the town grew and became a significant stopping point for travelers. The road that stretched from Baltimore to Gettysburg and Hanover, Pennsylvania, traversed this settlement and gave rise to such businesses as Forney's Tavern, known for its hospitality and good food. While the road brought prosperity, to some it foretold times of growth and change. In 1804, Jacob Medairy sought to block this progress by constructing a house in its path. Roadbuilders simply went around the house, and this deflection has been preserved over time. Look for it at the junction of Reisterstown Road (M–140) and Cockeys Mill Road.

Progress continued to take precedence over preservation as new houses, gas stations, and businesses were constructed in this busy corridor. Despite the low profile of the town's historic beginnings, there remains a sense of its presence. At the bend in the road is **Beckley's Blacksmith Shop** and the **Polly Reister House,** a two-and-a-half-story brick building with a one-story wing, erected in

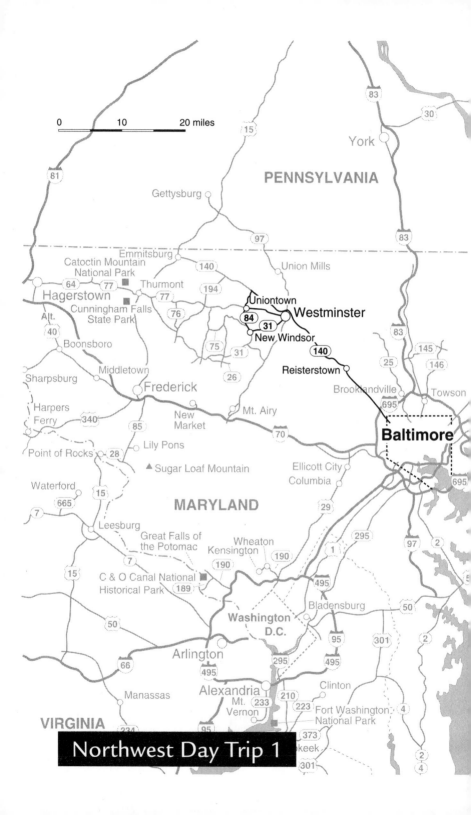

0   10   20 miles

81

PENNSYLVANIA

York

Gettysburg

15

83

30

97

83

Emmitsburg

Catoctin Mountain
National Park

140

Union Mills

64   77   Thurmont

Hagerstown

77

194

Uniontown   Westminster

84

83

145

Cunningham Falls
State Park

76

31

146

Alt.
40

75

New Windsor

25

Boonsboro

31

26

140

Middletown

Reisterstown

Sharpsburg

Frederick

Brooklandville

695

Towson

Harpers
Ferry   340

85

New
Market

Mt. Airy

70

Baltimore

Point of Rocks   28

Lily Pons

Ellicott City

Columbia

695

Waterford

15

665

MARYLAND

29

7

Leesburg

Great Falls of
the Potomac

Wheaton

295

97

2

Kensington

190

1

15

C & O Canal National
Historical Park

190

189

495

Bladensburg

50

Washington
D.C.

95

301

2

50

295

495

Arlington

495

Clinton

66

Manassas

Alexandria

210

223   Fort Washington
National Park

4

Mt.
Vernon

233

VIRGINIA

234

95

373

keek

301

2
4

Northwest Day Trip 1

1779. The **Henry Weist House** is located at 410 Main Street. Erected in 1773, it is constructed of stone and stucco and is indicative of the architectural style of the local area. Returning to Cockeys Mill Road, drive a short distance to the **Reisterstown Cemetery.** Originally developed around a log cabin that was used for Lutheran religious services as early as 1765, it is the resting place for early town residents and local soldiers and patriots of the Revolutionary War.

WESTMINSTER, MD

William Winchester, an English immigrant, bought more than one hundred acres of land in 1754 for 150 pounds or about $4.50 per acre. Later, he named the property Westminster in memory of his British birthplace. The town quickly became a trading center for the bounty from the rich farmland around it and a stopping-off point for wagons traveling between the grain fields of central Pennsylvania and the Port of Baltimore. When Carroll County was created in 1837, the city's central location and its zealous advocates helped secure its designation as the county seat.

The strategic location and bountiful resources of Westminster lent themselves well to the needs of the Union and Confederate troops during the Civil War. Both forces occupied the town three times within three years. Although the town was active in supplying resources, no significant battle action occurred here. The town, suffering little, returned easily to peacetime activities.

Westminster remains a peaceful, country town that is truly a pleasure to visit. Many of its fine buildings are included in the National Register of Historic Places. The town center is charming with its preserved eighteenth-century homes. Today's visitors will delight in the variety of specialty shops among the historic sites.

From Reisterstown continue northeast on M–140 to Westminster.

WHERE TO GO

Walking Tours. Located at 210 East Main Street. Stop first at the visitors information center to pick up literature on local attractions and specific information on the walking tours. The **Court Street and Court Square Walking Tour**'s theme is that of planned city development coupled respectfully with preservation of the old. The tour incorporates examples of early American architecture, an 1846 Episcopal Church and graveyard, the 1837 Old Jail, and the Pennsylvania-Georgian-style courthouse. The tour takes approximately one hour. Free. Call for a reservation: (410) 848-1388.

The **Architectural Walking Tour of Historic Westminster** incorporates a variety of architectural styles and interesting facades, and it can be extended to take in the downtown shopping area. The tour takes approximately one and one-half hours. Free. (800) 272-1933.

While both of these self-guided walking tours are free, arrangements for guided tours for groups of ten or more may be made for a reasonable fee.

The Carroll County Visitors Center welcomes your requests for additional information at (800) 272-1933 or by writing 210 East Main Street, Westminster, MD 21157. While visiting the county information center in Westminster, be sure to pick up the walking tour guide for Uniontown—the next destination in this county on our day trip itinerary.

Sherman-Fisher-Shellman House. Located at 210 East Main Street. Having begun your visit to Westminster at the visitors center, you are already standing in this town house (c. 1800), which also serves as the headquarters of the Historical Society of Carroll County. The house contains administrative offices, a genealogical research library, **Miss Carroll's Childrens Shop** (a permanent doll and toy exhibit), and an auditorium for lectures and receptions. By appointment. Fee. (410) 848-6494.

Carroll County Farm Museum. Located at 500 South Center Street. The entrance is located between M-32 and M-27. If you hurry through this fascinating attraction, chances are you'll miss the bonus that comes with taking your time and soaking up the pervasive feeling of the nineteenth-century farming lifestyle. The main house of this living museum was built in 1852 and offers today's visitors six rooms on display with authentic furnishings. The outbuildings house a variety of self-directed tours and displays.

The museum buildings are surrounded by 140 acres of open space with a lake, picnic tables, large shade trees, and nature trails.

The area comes alive with historical functions during harvest days and festivals scheduled each year, especially during the Maryland Wine Festival. (See Festivals and Celebrations at the back of the book.) Free parking is provided. Fee. (410) 848-7775 or (800) 654-4645.

WHERE TO EAT

Baugher's Country Restaurant and Farm Orchard Market. At the junction of M-31 and M-32 (Main Street) in Westminster. This combination restaurant, market, and bakery features a selection ranging from steaks to Eastern Shore seafood, plus homemade baked goods and ice cream. You can also pick your own fruits and vegetables here. $; ☐. (410) 848-7413.

Maria's Restaurant. Located at 532 Baltimore Boulevard (M-140). Maria's features a variety of fare including seafood, steaks, pasta, and pizza. $$; ☐. Lunch and dinner. (410) 848-5666.

Cockey's Tavern. Located at 216 East Main Street. Fresh seafood is the specialty here. Sample lobster, fish, and crabs at their best. Also, don't miss the homemade soups and pies. $$-$$$; ☐. (410) 848-4202.

WHERE TO SHOP

The Carroll County Farmer's Market. Located at the Carroll County Agricultural Center, Smith Avenue, in Westminster. Parking is adjacent to the Farm Museum. Be sure to sample the homemade baked goods, fresh fruits and vegetables, meats, seafood, and eggs. Other offerings include crafts, flowers, shrubs, and free weekly demonstrations by local artists. Open most Saturdays June to September, and for special Easter, spring, and Christmas markets, from 8:00 A.M. to 1:00 P.M. Be sure to call ahead for specific dates. Call (410) 848-7748, (410) 875-2158, or (800) 272-1933.

UNIONTOWN, MD

This country village is one of the oldest in Carroll County, dating from the late eighteenth century. It is situated on a large tract of land once known as the "Orchard." Uniontown was a prosperous business community prior to the Civil War, but when the Western Maryland Railroad bypassed Uniontown, it forged the area's future as a quiet, rural spot, untouched by commercialism.

At the west end of town, which is the oldest part, there are several large brick homes that were built in the early 1800s. These houses were the taverns and the hotel of the earlier village. Today they are preserved and occupied by private citizens of the town.

There have been few changes here since the late nineteenth century. Uniontown is still the quaint, peaceful village it was then. In 1970, it was designated a Historic District.

Visitors may delight in the number of antiques shops in the area. Merchants here specialize in handcrafts, antique furniture, and handmade reproductions. Be sure to visit the country store and town post office located in the center of town. Call (410) 848-7903.

From Westminster, continue west on M-140 to Royer Road. Turn left and continue to Uniontown Road. Then, drive 6 miles on Uniontown Road to Uniontown.

WHERE TO GO

Uniontown Walking Tour. Pick up the walking tour to Uniontown at the visitors information center, 210 East Main Street. The free tour of the historic district takes about one hour. To get more information, request walking tours by mail, or arrange for a guided group tour, call or write the Carroll County Office of Tourism, 125 North Court Street, Westminster, MD 21157. Call (410) 848-1388 or (800) 272-1933.

NEW WINDSOR, MD

Settled in the early nineteenth century, the town was formerly called Sulphur Springs. It was renamed New Windsor in 1844 and today boasts a unique International Gift Shop, one of the largest of four such nonprofit outlets for artisans' crafts in the country.

From Uniontown, drive south on M-84 to New Windsor at the junction of M-31.

WHERE TO GO

The International Gift Shop. Located in the New Windsor Service Center, Main Street at M-31. A Church of the Brethren program, the gift shop showcases the art and quality handcrafts of more than forty countries.

Here artisans produce attractive items using the skills of their heritage and the materials of their country. Revenues from the sale of these indigenous crafts are channeled both to the artisan and to the procurement of clothing and medical supplies for the contributing country, helping to build vital links from one culture to another. A cafeteria-style dining room is on the premises. Call (410) 635-8711.

For return routing to Baltimore, drive east on M–31 to Westminster. Then drive east on M–140 to Baltimore. Or, if time permits, continue driving west on M–140 to Emmitsburg for the first stop in Day Trip 2 of this chapter.

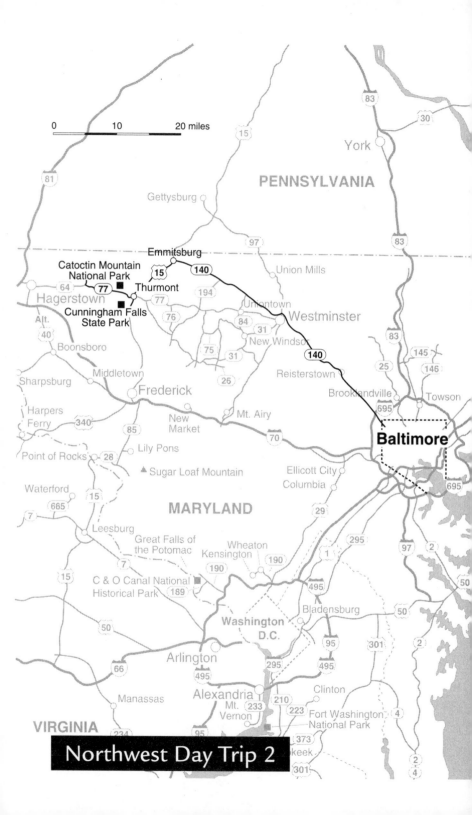

Northwest Day Trip 2

EMMITSBURG, MD

This rural community, just 11 miles south of Gettysburg, is of special interest to visitors of the Catholic faith. Tucked into the beautifully forested foothills of western Maryland is the first National Catholic Shrine in the United States: a replica of the Grotto of Lourdes. Also in Emmitsburg is the peaceful retreat of Mother Elizabeth Ann Seton—the first American-born saint. Abounding in nature's beauty and bountiful quiet areas for meditation, this Maryland landmark is a worthy, experiential venture.

From Baltimore, drive northwest on M–140 to Westminster, through Taneytown to Emmitsburg. Turn left at the town square and drive ½ mile to the Seton Shrines.

WHERE TO GO

The Seton Shrine Center. Located at 333 South Seton Avenue, Emmitsburg. Visitors are directed first to the Seton Shrine Center for an orientation to the self-guided tours on the "Seton Way." Visitors are requested to maintain the atmosphere of quiet retreat and meditation. A brief slide presentation highlights the historical sites at the shrine. Free. Contributions are accepted. Ample free parking and a gift shop are located nearby. (301) 447–6606.

Saint Elizabeth Ann Seton (Mother Seton) was the founder of the religious order of the Sisters of Charity and is now canonized as the first American-born saint.

Married to William Seton at the age of twenty, she bore him five children. When widowed in 1803, she turned to the Catholic

Church for solace and converted to Catholicism in 1805. She went on to become a nun in 1808 and opened a school in Baltimore. After receiving the title of "Mother" in 1809, she migrated to Emmitsburg, where she established the order of the Sisters of Charity and the first parochial school in the United States. Mother Seton died in Emmitsburg in 1821, was beatified in 1963, and was canonized in 1975.

The National Shrine Grotto of Lourdes. Grotto Road, off US-15 in Emmitsburg. This tribute to the Catholic faith is the oldest replica of Lourdes Grotto in the Western Hemisphere. Stations of the cross are beautifully placed along a natural, garden path to the Grotto. Open year-round from dawn to dusk. Regularly scheduled services are held from Easter to November 1 each year.

WHERE TO EAT

Carriage House Inn. Located at 200 South Seton Avenue, Emmitsburg. This dining spot features seafood, steak, and homemade desserts for lunch and dinner. $-$$; ☐. (301) 447-2366.

THURMONT, MD

Thurmont is a small, rural town immediately adjacent to the Catoctin Mountain National Park and the Cunningham Falls State Park. The original settlement dates back to 1751 when the Jacob Weller family built their homestead here after abandoning a wagon train headed west. The Wellers established several small industries here, and the town became known as Mechanicstown during the early years. When the railroad was built nearby, the area became easily accessible to city folks seeking a mountain retreat. The magnificent scenery and high altitude made the area a popular resort, and it was renamed Thurmont, "gateway to the mountains."

From Emmitsburg, drive south on the Catoctin Mountain Highway (US-15) to Thurmont.

WHERE TO GO

The Catoctin Mountain Zoo. This natural attraction is located a short distance south of the town of Thurmont, on US-15, near the entrance to the Cunningham Falls State Park. Selected endangered species and exhibits of 300 animals are displayed amid green, mountainside surroundings. Special animal shows are arranged during May through September. Open April through October. Fee. For more information regarding exhibits and special events, call (301) 271-3180.

CATOCTIN MOUNTAIN NATIONAL PARK

From Thurmont proper, drive a short distance south on US-15 to M-77. Turn right and drive west to the park entrance. Just off M-77 is the Visitors Information Center, which offers details on park programs and facilities. Adjacent to the center is a small display area that highlights the cultural and natural histories of the area and its recreational activities. The center and exhibits are free. (301) 663-9330.

Facilities and recreational opportunities are spread among 5,769 acres of magnificent mountainside and are administered by the National Park Service. The park's name was derived from the Kittocton Indian tribe that once lived at the foot of the mountains near the Potomac River.

After picking up your free pocket map guide to the park at the visitors center, begin your survey of things to see and do. A self-guided auto tour along 7 miles of the back roads of the Catoctin ridge begins at the intersection of Park Central Road and Manahan Road and follows a route of scenic and historic interest.

A developed picnic area is located on Owens Creek and offers modern restrooms, tables, fireplaces, and trash receptacles. Self-guiding walking trails are designated throughout the park; leaflets available at the trailheads describe nature along the routes. Hiking, cross-country skiing, and snowshoeing are readily available for the hardier visitor. About 25 miles of well-marked trails, such as Wolf Rock and Thurmont Vista, traverse the park to outstanding views and natural wonders. Parking areas are provided at the trailheads. For more specific information regarding all recreational facilities and for an advance mailing of the park guide map, call (301) 663-9330.

OF SPECIAL INTEREST

Camp David, the mountain retreat of American presidents since Franklin D. Roosevelt, is located here just off the Park Central Road. It is closed to the public.

Blue Blazes Still. Situated within walking distance from the visitors center in the park is a genuine still that was relocated here from the Smoky Mountains after Prohibition days. It is operated by the National Park Service as an interpretive program. Free. Sorry, no samples! (301) 663-9330.

Owens Creek Campground is open from mid-April through the third Sunday of November and features modern restrooms, tables, and fireplaces.

CUNNINGHAM FALLS STATE PARK

M-77 runs east and west, right through the middle of the Catoctin Mountain and Cunningham Falls parks. So, your visit to this area has a double bonus as you select from the scenery and fun in each park. The 4,950 acres in Cunningham Falls State Park are distributed between two separate recreation areas: the **Manor Area,** located on the park's eastern boundary near US-15, and the **William Houck Area,** located just 3 miles west of Thurmont, off M-77 on Catoctin Hollow Road. Keep these separated sites in mind so that you easily locate the recreational facility you choose.

The State Park office at the William Houck Area is open year-round. An information kiosk located at the Manor Area is open on weekends from April through October. Two developed picnic areas are provided at the Manor and William Houck areas and have restrooms, tables, fireplaces, and trash receptacles. No fires are permitted when picnicking elsewhere in the park.

Two nature-oriented walking trails are the Cunningham Falls Trail and the Renaissance Trail. Descriptive leaflets are available at the trailheads. Hiking, cross-country skiing, and snowshoeing are especially good on Cat Rock Trail; there is a parking area at the trailhead.

Camping at the William Houck Campground and the Manor Campground is available from mid-April through October for families. Restrooms, tables, and fireplaces are provided.

Swimming, fishing, and boating are available on Hunting Creek Lake, which has two sandy beaches, a modern bathhouse, and a concession building. The lake is stocked with fish, and a Maryland fishing license with trout stamp is required for persons sixteen years of age and older. Stream fishing in Owens Creek, Big Hunting Creek, and Little Hunting Creek is also regulated by the state of Maryland. Canoes may be rented during the summer and fall.

Cunningham Falls State Park is administered by the Maryland Park Service. Park headquarters are located at the William Houck Area. For more information regarding facilities and recreational opportunities or for an advance mailing of the park map and guide, call (301) 271-7574.

OF SPECIAL INTEREST

The Catoctin Iron Furnace. Located in the southeastern tip of the Cunningham Falls State Park, on M-806 at Catoctin Hollow Road. This massive stone furnace, vintage 1771, smelted ore for shells used in the Battle of Yorktown and continued to function until 1905. The stone cottages of the original iron workers are situated nearby. Free.

From Cunningham Falls State Park, continue south on US-15 to Frederick, where you can explore the opportunities described in Day Trip 2 of the West section. If time doesn't permit this extended itinerary, pick up I-70 east out of Frederick to US-40 east to Baltimore. Or, simply reverse your routing on this day trip by driving northeast on US-15 into Thurmont and Emmitsburg. From Emmitsburg, drive southeast on M-140 into Baltimore.

WHERE TO EAT

Cozy Restaurant. Located at 103 Frederick Road, M-806, Thurmont. The pride of Frederick County is this unusual restaurant with ten dining rooms (seating capacity near 700). The well-served family fare is varied American cuisine. For lunch and dinner each day of the week, Cozy prepares a groaning board with more than sixty items plus a do-it-yourself ice cream sundae bar. Also a country breakfast buffet on Saturday and Sunday. Children's prices available and sandwiches served anytime. $-$$; ☐. (301) 271-7373.

The Mountain Gate Family Restaurant. Located at 133 Frederick Road, Thurmont. Excellent, homestyle cooking served in a comfortable environment. No alcoholic beverages served. $; ☐. (301) 271-4373.

The Shamrock Restaurant. US-15 and Fitzgerald Road, Thurmont. Excellent seafood and salad are served in a friendly manner amid the Irish decor. $-$$; ☐. (301) 271-2912.

WHERE TO SHOP

The Cozy Shops. Adjacent to the Cozy Restaurant are a series of quaint shops featuring another groaning board of items. **The General Store** at 106 Frederick Road is a linen and candy outlet, and it also offers jams and jellies, pewter, tins, candles, soaps, crafts, and much more. Call (301) 271-4301. **The Doll House** at 102 Frederick Road boasts dolls for all ages at all prices. Call (301) 271-3430. **The Cozy Antiques and Trivia Shop** at 101 Frederick Road invites you to stop and browse at your leisure among the assorted treasures. Call (301) 271-3245. And, **The Floral Shop** at 104 Frederick Road makes arrangements for any occasion and features a Christmas Shoppe. Call (301) 271-2445.

The Gateway Orchard Farm Market and Candyland. Just ½ mile north of Thurmont on US-15 is a unique combination attraction featuring farm-fresh produce all year. The proprietor recommends calling ahead for information regarding the availability of fruits or vegetables for canning or freezing. Gateway also carries more than one hundred varieties of candies, as well as bulk chocolates and flavorings to make your own recipes. Open seven days a week. Call (301) 271-2322.

Union Mills, MD
Gettysburg, PA

UNION MILLS, MD

Ah! Green grasses and golden crops woven around the contours of rolling hills. Dairy herds and horse farms tended by the dauntless vigil of endless white fences, and a friendliness that just comes natural to the folks who live here. Union Mills is set amid Carroll County's finest scenery. From Baltimore, drive north on Reisterstown Road (M–140). Immediately after passing Reisterstown, bear left onto the Westminster Pike (also M–140). At Westminster, turn right onto the Littlestown Pike (M–97) and drive north.

WHERE TO GO

The Union Mills Homestead. As you drive 7 miles north on M–97 from Westminster, the Homestead will be on your right. Also known as the **Shriver Homestead,** the main house is a weathered, gray clapboard dwelling facing the valley carved by Big Pipe Creek. The Homestead has been there through many stages of growth, beginning as four rooms in 1797. The early work of David and Andrew Shriver was soon outgrown and the homestead grew to twenty-three rooms to meet the needs of six generations of the Shriver family. Nearby, they constructed their brick grist and saw mill on Pipe Creek.

While it is doubtful that a visit to this attraction will completely convert you from occasional binges of closet cleaning, its unique fascination lies in the preserved, undisturbed, and well-utilized array of tools, toys, and furniture that spanned 150 years.

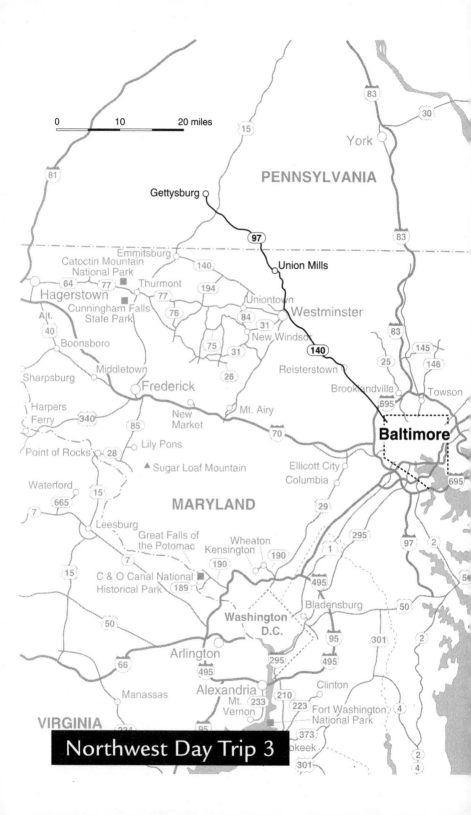

Northwest Day Trip 3

Virtually every item acquired by this family was retained and used. Seldom was anything destroyed. The antithesis of today's disposable society, the Shriver Homestead has a dual value. It is a tribute to the days when people repaired articles rather than replaced them, and further, it is a living documentation of American farm life. This site has been declared a National Historic Landmark. Fee. Call for hours. (410) 848-2288.

For more information about the Homestead and special events here during the year, write to 3311 Littlestown Pike, Westminster, MD 21157.

The Union Mills Grist Mill. Established adjacent to the Shriver Homestead on Big Pipe Creek, the old mill was constructed from more than 100,000 bricks that were handmade from clay found on the property. Water diverted from Big Pipe Creek powered the large undershot water wheel. In time, the brick grist mill became the focus of the Shriver brother–owned industrial complex. Together with a sawmill, cooper shop, blacksmith shop, and tannery, the enterprises became known as Union Mills.

Today, Union Mills grain products are stone-ground in the original brick grist mill of Andrew and David Shriver built in 1797. Fee. (410) 848-2288.

GETTYSBURG, PA

One of the greatest battles ever fought on this continent and one of the most decisive battles of world history took place here, in Gettysburg.

The Battle of Gettysburg began on July 1, 1863. Here, General Robert E. Lee's Confederate Army of 75,000 men met the 97,000-man Union Army of General George G. Meade. Confederates attacked the Northern troops through July 2, driving their opponents through Gettysburg to the heights south of town. However, the strength of this new position, coupled with Lee's poorly coordinated strategies, caused the Confederates to fail. There were enormous losses on both sides. On July 3, Lee made the fateful decision to attack the center of Meade's position on Cemetery Ridge. The Union defenders saw 15,000 Confederate soldiers lined shoulder to shoulder 1½ miles from end to end. In fifty minutes, 10,000 of the 15,000 men in the assault became casualties. With the failure of the attack, known as Pickett's Charge, the battle was over—the Union was preserved. There were 51,000 casualties altogether, making Gettysburg one of the bloodiest battles of American history.

From Union Mills, continue northwest on M–97 across the Maryland-Pennsylvania border. Continue now on P–97 (designated the Baltimore Pike) directly into Gettysburg.

WHERE TO GO

Visitor Center. Continue along the Baltimore Pike and enter the Gettysburg National Military Park. (The Baltimore Pike becomes Baltimore Street as it exits the park and enters Gettysburg proper.) To reach the Visitor Center, turn left off of the Baltimore Pike onto Hunt Avenue at Meade's Headquarters. Then turn right and drive north on Taneytown Road to the ample, free parking adjacent to the Visitor Center. You can also enter this area from Steinwehr Avenue. Begin your visit here for orientation and information and current events schedules. You will also find a large collection of Civil War artifacts and licensed guides here. The Electric Map orientation program is a thirty-minute re-creation of the Battle of Gettysburg on a large relief map with colored lights and narration. Admission is free to the Visitor Center. A fee is charged for the Electric Map. (717) 334-6100.

Cyclorama Center. Adjacent to the Visitor Center is the large (356 by 26 feet) painting of Pickett's Charge. Completed by artist Paul Philippoteaux in 1884, the painting is displayed with a dramatic sound and light show. The Cyclorama Center also has tour information and exhibits. A fee is charged to view the painting. (717) 334-6100.

Self-Guided Auto Tour. This suggested 15-mile route begins at the Cyclorama Center and ends at the National Cemetery. Allow two hours to complete the tour. A free map and guidebook are available at the Visitor Center and the Cyclorama Center. Roads are open from 6:00 A.M. to 10:00 P.M., daily. (717) 334-6100.

Licensed Battlefield Guides. Originating from the Cyclorama Center, tour guides licensed by the National Park Service offer an opportunity for personal and in-depth tours of the battlefield. The two-hour tour accompanied by a guide is a good way to fully appreciate the events of Gettysburg. Fee. (717) 334-6100.

National Civil War Wax Museum. Steinwehr Avenue, Gettysburg. Well, if you didn't catch the whole story in the larger-than-life presentations at the Battlefield Park, stop here for all you ever wanted to know about Pickett's Charge. An animated figure of President Lincoln presents the Gettysburg Address. Fee. Call for hours. (717) 334-6245.

Soldiers National Museum. Located on Baltimore Street, adjacent to A. Lincoln's Place. On display here are dioramas of the Civil War; life-size, animated human interest "Vignettes of History"; and an extensive collection of Civil War relics. Some visitors may remember that this collection was formerly Charley Weaver's Museum, named for the lovable character played by Cliff Arquette, a dedicated Civil War historian and actor. Fee. (717) 334-4890.

Old Gettysburg Village of Quaint Shops. Located on Baltimore Street across from the Gettysburg Tour Center, this is an opportunity to escape from the memories of the ravages of the Civil War into a nostalgic visit to the past. A gift shop, country store, Amish shop, and ice cream store afford a shopping spree of treats and treasures.

The list of attractions in this area goes on and on with much of the focus on the Civil War. It is a fascinating destination on this day trip and one that may entice you to stay for an overnight visit. The Gettysburg Travel Council welcomes requests for information on the many attractions. Write 35 Carlisle Street, Gettysburg, PA 17325, or call (717) 334-6274.

From Gettysburg, return to Baltimore by reversing the route of this day trip. Or, if time permits, you may want to pick up the York Pike (US-30) off of York Street in Gettysburg. From here, drive east into Lancaster, Pennsylvania, to sample the special Pennsylvania Dutch country described in Day Trip 3 of the North section of this book. I-83 south becomes the most expedient route to Baltimore from here.

WHERE TO EAT

General Lee's Family Restaurant. West US-30. Country cooking in an early American atmosphere. Don't miss the famous farm desserts! $-$$; ☐. (717) 334-2200.

Farnsworth House Inn. Located at 401 Baltimore Street. This Victorian bed and breakfast offers the opportunity to dine among authentic Civil War decor and artifacts (including bullet holes!). It features period specialties, steaks, and seafood and contains a museum and gift/print gallery. $$; ☐. (717) 334–8838.

The Dobbin House Restaurant. Located at 89 Steinwehr Avenue, Gettysburg. Early American cuisine is served here in this authentic colonial tavern (1776). Children's menu available. $$–$$$; ☐. Reservations are advised. (717) 334–2100.

WHERE TO STAY

Quality Inn, Gettysburg Motor Lodge. Located at 380 Steinwehr Avenue. Located in town, it is 1 mile south of Center Square in Gettysburg. Ninety rooms, a heated pool, a cocktail lounge, and a putting green are among the amenities offered by the inn and lodge. It is within walking distance of restaurants, tours, and museums in the historic area. ☐. Call (717) 334–1103.

Directory

FESTIVALS AND CELEBRATIONS

THE GREAT OUTDOORS

AERIAL SPORTS

WATER SPORTS

HIKING AND CYCLING

SEASONAL INFORMATION

REGIONAL INFORMATION

Festivals and Celebrations

JANUARY

MARYLAND
Annapolis. Opening Day, Maryland General Assembly. The annual ninety-day legislative session begins with opening ceremonies in the State House. (410) 841–3810.

PENNSYLVANIA
Philadelphia. Mummers Parade. A world-famous parade of 30,000 brightly costumed Mummers, string bands, and comics. (215) 336–3050.

VIRGINIA
Alexandria. Lee Birthday Celebration. Joint celebration of the birthdays of "Light Horse Harry" Lee and his son, Robert E. Lee. (703) 548–8454.

FEBRUARY

MARYLAND
Hydes. Valentine's Day Celebration. Treat yourself to an afternoon of wine tastings, gourmet hors d'oeuvres, and winery tours at Boordy Vineyards. (410) 592–5015.

VIRGINIA
Alexandria. George Washington Birthday Parade. See the nation's largest parade celebrating the birthday of George Washington. (703) 838–4200.

Alexandria. Revolutionary War Encampment and Skirmish. Re-enactments of Revolutionary and British eighteenth-century military camps with staged battle skirmishes. (703) 838-4200.

WEST VIRGINIA
Berkeley Springs. Nineteenth-Century Dance and Music Workshop. Cacapon Resort State Park. Workshops in country dance and clogging and demonstrations of nineteenth-century banjo and old-time fiddle playing. (800) CALL WVA.
Berkeley Springs. A Toast to the Tap. International Water Tasting and Winter Festival of The Waters. In this colonial town, originally known as Bath for its curative spring waters, this is a juried tasting of the world's best waters. (304) 258-9147 or (800) 447-8797.

MARCH

MARYLAND
Thurmont. Maple Syrup Demonstrations. Tree-tapping, sap-boiling, and maple products for sale. Interpretations are given by the park ranger along with instructive films. (301) 271-7574.
Timonium. Greenberg's Great Train, Doll House, and Toy Show. Visit 300 booths featuring operating train layouts, furnished doll-house displays, and workshops. (410) 795-7447.
Annapolis. Annual St. Patrick's Day Green Beer Race. Starts at Second and Severn Streets in Eastport and finishes at Marmadukes Pub. Awards for fastest runner, best costume, and others. (410) 269-5420.
Coltons Point. Maryland Day. Celebrate the founding of Maryland with a wreath-laying ceremony, entertainment, and refreshments. (301) 769-2222.
St. Mary's City. Maryland Days Weekend. Celebration of the founding of Maryland with exhibits, crafts demonstrations, waterfront displays, southern Maryland seafood, bluegrass, gospel, and period music, and a symbolic session of the Maryland Assembly in the Old State House. (301) 862-0960.

PENNSYLVANIA
Philadelphia. Philadelphia Flower Show. Philadelphia County Civic Center. Celebrate the coming of spring at the world's largest indoor flower show. (215) 823-7400.

VIRGINIA

Mount Vernon. Annual Needlework Exhibit. More than 2,000 international needlework entries are displayed at the Woodlawn Plantation. Demonstrations. (703) 780–4000.

APRIL

MARYLAND

Accokeek. National Colonial Farm Day. Demonstrations and exhibits of eighteenth-century colonial agriculture and domestic life. (301) 283–2113.

Maryland. Maryland House and Garden Pilgrimage. Important houses and gardens throughout the state are opened to visitors. (410) 821–6933.

Sharpsburg. Easter Sunrise Service. Sunrise service at approximately 5:30 A.M. at Antietam Battlefield. Sponsored by the combined churches of Sharpsburg. (301) 432–5124.

St. Leonard. Southern Maryland Celtic Festival and Highland Gathering. Celebrate the Celtic heritage of England, Ireland, Scotland, and Wales with competitions, dance, food, and merchandise. (410) 257–9003.

PENNSYLVANIA

Chadds Ford. Brandywine River Museum Antiques Show. Chadds Ford–Brandywine River Museum. Thirty of America's top dealers show fine decorative objects and furniture. (610) 388–2700.

VIRGINIA

Arlington. Easter Sunrise Service, Arlington National Cemetery. The service is conducted by chaplains of several denominations with music provided by the Army Chorus and the Marine Corps Band. (703) 521–0072.

Leesburg. Oatlands Point-to-Point. Thoroughbred races at Oatlands Manor House and tours of the mansion are scheduled. (703) 777–3174.

WEST VIRGINIA

Harpers Ferry, Martinsburg, and Shepherdstown. House and Garden Tour of Charles Town. This annual tour represents every era in American history. (304) 725–4886.

MAY

MARYLAND
Howard County Fairgrounds. Maryland Sheep and Wool Festival. Crafts, shearing, and weaving demonstrations. (410) 531-3647.
Towson. Towsontowne Spring Festival. A mammoth festival that covers most of the downtown area. Five stages with continuous entertainment, food, crafts, plants, rides. (410) 825-1144.
Queen Anne's Bridge Walk Rendezvous. Chesapeake Bay Business Park. Music, food, crafts, and the annual public walk across the Chesapeake Bay Bridge. A traditional favorite event. (410) 643-8530.
Baltimore. Preakness Festival Stakes. Pimlico Race Course. A full week's agenda of fun and events leading to the famous race. (410) 542-9400.

PENNSYLVANIA
Chadds Ford. Colonial Military Re-enactment. Re-creation of an eighteenth-century military camp with demonstrations of typical drills and colonial crafts, all staged at the Brandywine Battlefield State Park. (610) 459-3342.
Gettysburg. Memorial Day Parade and Service. Holiday parade and commemorative services are scheduled. (717) 334-6274.
Gettysburg. Adams County Apple Blossom Festival. Orchard tours, crafts show, agricultural exhibits, apple butter boil, and plenty of home cookin' make this a "must do" for May. South Mountain Fair Grounds (10 miles north of Gettysburg). (717) 334-6374.

VIRGINIA
Arlington. Memorial Day Service, Arlington National Cemetery. Presidential wreath-laying at the Tomb of the Unknowns. (717) 521-0772.

JUNE

MARYLAND
Baltimore, Fort McHenry. National Flag Day Celebrations. Includes the world's largest living flag created by schoolchildren. Pause for the Pledge Ceremonies, patriotic music, and fireworks. (410) 563-3524.

Smallwood State Park. Revolutionary War Days. A re-created encampment, with actors, musicians, and craftsmen practicing the arts of the era. (800) 784–5380.

PENNSYLVANIA

Gettysburg. Civil War Heritage Days. Beginning in late June and extending into July is a nine-day Living History Encampment featuring authentic Civil War encampment, band concerts, Civil War lecture series, collectors' show, and book fair. Contact: Gettysburg Travel Council, 35 Carlisle Street, Gettysburg, PA 17325. (717) 334–6274.

Kennett Square. Illuminated Fountain Displays at Longwood Gardens are planned from June through August and include garden concerts. Contact: Longwood Gardens, US–1, Kennett Square, PA 19348. (610) 388–6741.

VIRGINIA

Alexandria. Alexandria Red Cross Waterfront Festival. Tall ships, marine exhibits, 10K race, fireworks, food, and boat races. Contact: Festival Office, 401 Duke Street, Alexandria, VA 22314. (703) 549–8300.

WEST VIRGINIA

Shepherdstown. The Great Rumsey Raft Race. Homemade-open-unlimited, rubber raft, canoe, and kayak races on the Potomac River. Contact: Eastern Gateway Travel Council, P.O. Box A, Harpers Ferry, WV 25425. (304) 535–2482.

Near Harpers Ferry. Spring Mountain Heritage Arts and Crafts Festival. Hundreds of selected craftspeople, folk dancing, and country and bluegrass music. (304) 725–2055 or (800) 624–0577.

JULY

MARYLAND

Baltimore. Artscape–Mt. Royal Avenue. An annual urban weekend celebration of the literary, performing, and visual arts. Several stages and top name entertainers. (410) 396–4575.

Westminster. Old-Fashioned July Fourth Celebration. Family outing at Carroll County Farm Museum with picnic basket auction, children's games, good food, and country crafts. Fireworks are scheduled after dark. (410) 876–2667.

Annapolis. Fourth of July Celebration. Features a Navy Band performance followed by fireworks over the harbor at dusk. (410) 263-7940.

Fair Hill. Cecil County Fair. Fair Hill Natural Resources Area. A complete county fair in a beautiful rural setting reminiscent of the English countryside. (410) 398-1867 or (410) 392-3440.

Westminster. Deer Creek Fiddlers Convention. Carroll County Farm Museum. A day-long bluegrass festival featuring some of the region's very best old-time bluegrass country groups. (410) 876-2667, (800) 654-4645.

PENNSYLVANIA

Kutztown. Kutztown Folk Festival. This event is a Pennsylvania Dutch extravaganza featuring indigenous cooking, crafts, music, and entertainment. The tiny town opens its heart and doors annually to the thousands of visitors who celebrate this event. (215) 683-8707.

Philadelphia. Welcome America Liberty Lighted Boat Parade. Penn's Landing, Delaware River. The Fourth of July is celebrated with a parade of decorated, illuminated boats and name entertainers. (215) 636-1666 or (800) 537-7676.

VIRGINIA

Alexandria. Annual Virginia Scottish Games. Highland dancing, bagpipe bands, animal demonstrations, sports, and good food. (703) 838-4200.

AUGUST

MARYLAND

Havre de Grace. Seafood Festival. All you can eat: crabs, clams, fish, oysters, salads, watermelon, and more. (410) 939-2877.

Crownsville. Maryland Renaissance Festival. Beginning in late August and extending into October, this festival features entertainers, crafts, games, and people in costumes of the sixteenth century. Ten stages, 230 performers, 145 craft shops. Open on weekends and Labor Day. (410) 266-7304, (800) 296-7304.

Cordova. St. Joseph Horse Show and Jousting Tournament. St. Joseph's Church. Features a morning horse show, afternoon country ham and barbecue chicken dinner, and jousting tournament. (410) 822-6915.

Carroll County. Old-Fashioned Corn Roast Festival. Union Mills Homestead. Features the local harvest favorites with roasted corn, tomatoes, and Maryland fried chicken. (410) 848–2288.

Hagerstown. Jonathan Hager Frontier Craft Days. Hager House and City Park. A weekend festival of arts, crafts, great country foods in season, bluegrass music, tours. (301) 739–8393.

Timonium. Maryland State Fair. Maryland State Fairgrounds. Thoroughbred horse racing, livestock demonstrations and judging, 4H displays, giant midway, county booths, farm crafts, and food judging. (410) 252–0200, ext. 226.

VIRGINIA

Alexandria. Eighteenth-century Fair. Eighteenth-century tavern life re-created with food, drink, demonstrations, music, and children's activities. Contact: Gadsby's Tavern Museum, 134 North Royal Street, Alexandria, VA 22314. (703) 838–4242.

Leesburg. August Court Days. Re-enactment of eighteenth-century court term with crafts, musicians, and dancers. (703) 777–0579.

Middleburg. Annual Virginia Wine Festival. Wine-tasting, grape-stomping, vineyard tours, and seminars. Contact: Vinifera Wine Growers Association, Box P, The Plains, VA 22171. (703) 754–8564.

Manassas. Civil War Re-enactment. Living history camps, skirmish, and major battle, Civil War fashion show, crafts, and bluegrass music. (703) 368–4813.

SEPTEMBER

MARYLAND

Boonsboro. Boonsborough Days. More than one hundred craftsmen featuring crafts show and sale, antiques, country store, entertainment, and food. (301) 432–5889.

New Market. New Market Days. Country food, buggy rides, historical displays, and entertainment. (301) 865–3926.

Westminster. Maryland Wine Festival. Sample Maryland wines from more than a dozen Maryland vineyards and fine cuisine at the Carroll County Farm Museum. This festival also features continuous entertainment and top-quality crafts. Winemaking seminars and judging. (410) 876–2667.

Westminster. Steam Show Days. Carroll County Farm Museum. An extravaganza of working antique farm equipment and antique cars. Working demonstrations, hayrides, flea market, farmhouse tours. (410) 876–2667 or (800) 654–4645.

PENNSYLVANIA
Chadds Ford. Brandywine Battlefield Revolutionary Times Reenactment. Eighteenth-century military encampments and mock-battle demonstrations at the Brandywine Battlefield State Park. (610) 459–3342.
Chadds Ford. Chadds Ford Days. Eighteenth-century country fair, costumed colonial craftsmen, live music, hayrides, meadow games, and great food are on the days' agenda. Don't miss "pigge and pippins"—pork and apples! (610) 388–7376.

WEST VIRGINIA
Harpers Ferry. Mountain Heritage Arts and Crafts Festival. Crafts, Appalachian folk music, and festivities. (304) 725–2055.

OCTOBER

MARYLAND
Annapolis. Chesapeake Appreciation Days. Skipjack races, land exhibits, air show with antique aircraft, and great Maryland seafood make this a super annual event. (410) 280–0445.
Laurel. Maryland Million Day. Laurel Race Course. Twelve races featuring only Maryland-bred horses. The only million-dollar state stallion stakes. (410) 792–7775.
Princess Anne. Olde Princess Anne Days. Teackle Mansion. Tour historic homes with costumed guides in this quaint Southern colonial town. (410) 657–2238.
Frederick. Oktoberfest at Schifferstadt. Schifferstadt Museum. A traditional German-style harvest fest featuring German music, food and biergarten, and crafts in this community primarily settled by German immigrants. (301) 663–3885.
Fair Hill. Three Day Event and Carriage Driving Championships. Fair Hill Natural Resource Area, Elkton. Olympic-level equestrian events with a Festival in the Country Fair. (800) CECIL-95.

VIRGINIA

Mount Vernon. Annual Fall Festival of Needlework. Seminars, sherry, original kits, and tours. Contact: Woodlawn Plantation, P.O. Box 37, Mount Vernon, VA 22121. (703) 780-4000.

Waterford. Annual Waterford Homes Tour and Crafts Exhibit. National Historic Landmark village celebrates eighteenth-century style with music, demonstrations, and tours. Contact: Waterford Foundation, P.O. Box 142, Waterford, VA 22190. (703) 882-3085.

NOVEMBER

DELAWARE

Winterthur Museum and Gardens. Yuletide at Winterthur. Beginning in November and extending to the end of December, see twenty-one of the museum's rooms re-create traditions of early holiday entertainment. (302) 888-4600.

MARYLAND

Easton. Waterfowl Festival. Decorative and working decoys, waterfowl art, duck and goose calling contest, antique guns, and auction. One of the largest and varied wildfowl festivals anywhere. (410) 822-4567.

Westminster. Christmas open house. Tour the mansion rooms of the Carroll County Farm Museum decorated in preparation for a theme Christmas. (410) 876-2667 or (800) 654-4645.

Sugarloaf's Fall Gaithersburg Crafts Festival. One of the East Coast's largest, most successful crafts fairs with more than 500 professional artisans displaying their crafts in this annual pre-Christmas festival. (301) 990-1400.

Upper Marlboro. Winter Festival of Lights. Watkins Regional Park. This drive-through holiday display features more than 200,000 colored lights. Donations of canned goods are requested. (301) 699-2545.

PENNSYLVANIA

Chadds Ford. A wide variety of traditional experiences and seasonal events celebrate the Christmas holidays. Beginning in November and extending to January, model train gardens, decorated trees, and best-loved winter scenes painted by the Wyeth family are displayed at the Brandywine River Museum. (610) 459-1900.

Kennett Square. Chrysanthemum Festival. Fifteen thousand spectacular mums are displayed indoors, and a festival of musical performances and craft demonstrations is in the American harvest tradition at Longwood Gardens. (610) 388-6741.

VIRGINIA

Leesburg. Christmas at Oatlands. Authentic 1880s decorations adorn the plantation manor house. (703) 777-0519.

DECEMBER

MARYLAND

Annapolis. The Maryland Statehouse by Candlelight and Christmas in Annapolis. Open house tours, museum houses with special events, concerts, feasting, pub crawls, and caroling. Contact: Annapolis and Anne Arundel County Conference and Visitors Bureau. Located at 26 West Street, Annapolis, MD 21401. (410) 280-0445.

Ellicott City. Old-Fashioned Christmas Gardens. Trains and displays back to 1930s, HO-gauge model railroad depicting the first 13 miles of the B&O. (410) 461-1944.

Hagerstown. Miller House Christmas. Federal-period town houses decked in holiday decor of fresh greens, large Christmas trees. (301) 797-8782.

Havre de Grace. Havre de Grace Candlelight Tour. Tour of historic town, including museums, homes, and businesses. (410) 939-3947.

Inner Harbor, Baltimore. Baltimore's New Year's Eve Extravaganza. Nonalcoholic musical events at the Baltimore Convention center followed by a New Year countdown and fireworks display. Each year upwards of 200,000 people are on hand to celebrate. (410) 837-4636 or (800) 282-6632.

Historic Annapolis, various locations. First Night Annapolis. The city becomes a stage and celebrates the New Year with music, drama, and all forms of entertainment. (410) 268-8553.

PENNSYLVANIA

Kennett Square. Longwood Gardens Christmas Display. Get your Christmas spirit here! See more than 2,000 poinsettias in the heated conservatory and a magnificent Christmas tree exhibition. Outside, 35,000 lights adorn eighty trees. Music and choral concerts each evening. (610) 388-6471.

Ephrata. Ephrata Cloister. Live, theatrical improvisations of cloister life with period costumes. Special candlelight Christmas tour. (717) 733-4811.

Lancaster. Victorian Christmas at Wheatland. Candlelight tour of James Buchanan's historic 1828 mansion residence, decorated for the holidays in Victorian style. Tours by guides in period costumes. (717) 392-8721.

VIRGINIA

Alexandria. Scottish Christmas Walk. Parade with bagpipers and clans, concerts, house tours, antiques, and crafts displays are among the festivities. (703) 549-0111.

Alexandria. Old Town Christmas Candlelight Tour. Four historic properties are decorated for the holidays and open for tours. Refreshments and period music are planned. (703) 838-4200.

Lorton. Carols by Candlelight at Gunston Hall Plantation. Eighteenth-century music, caroling, and refreshments. (703) 550-9220.

Mount Vernon. Carols by Candlelight at Woodlawn Plantation. Nineteenth-century Yuletide musicians and madrigalists with period music. (703) 780-4000.

WEST VIRGINIA

Harpers Ferry National Historical Park. Old Tyme Christmas. Authentic celebration of the mid-1800s with natural decorations and music make this a worthwhile holiday event. (304) 535-6029 or (800) 848-TOUR.

The Great Outdoors

DELAWARE

Tourism and campground information is available from:

Delaware State Travel Service
99 Kings Highway
P.O. Box 1401
Dover, DE 19903
Phone (800) 441–8846

Boating and fishing information can be obtained from:

Division of Fish and Wildlife
99 Kings Highway
P.O. Box 1401
Dover, DE 19903
Phone (302) 739–4431

MARYLAND

Maps, winter activities, camping, hunting, and fishing information are available from:

Maryland Forest and Park Service
Department of Natural Resources
Tawes State Office Building
Annapolis, MD 21401
Phone (800) 825–7275

PENNSYLVANIA

General state park information, maps, and pamphlets relating to specific parks are available from:

Office of Public Information
Department of Environmental Resources

Harrisburg, PA 17120
Phone (717) 787-2657

VIRGINIA

Information is available at all Virginia Highway Information centers. Information and reservations are available from:

Department of Conservation & Recreation
203 Governor Street, Suite 302
Richmond, VA 23219
Phone (804) 786-1712

WASHINGTON, DC, AREA–MARYLAND– NATIONAL CAPITAL PARK AND PLANNING COMMISSION

For information, write:

Parkside Headquarters
9500 Brunett Avenue
Silver Spring, MD 20901

For park permits and information call (301) 588-7400.

WEST VIRGINIA

West Virginia Department of Natural Resources
Division of Parks and Recreation
State Capitol—SP
Charleston, WV 25305

For park and forest information, reservations, hunting and fishing information, and other data relating to outdoor recreation, call (304) 558-2764.

Aerial Sports

The first human ever to go aloft in the United States was a thirteen-year-old boy in a hot air balloon in Baltimore. Maryland's aviation history also boasts of having the Wright brothers teach flying at the College Park Airport.

Today, Maryland offers many exciting aerial opportunities, such as ballooning, hang gliding, helicoptering, light plane, parasailing, and soaring.

BALLOONING
The Chesapeake Balloon Association maintains a list of numerous pilots in Maryland who offer balloons for hire. (301) 869-2359. **Light Flight Hot Air Balloons** in Bel Air offers a "Champagne Charter Flight" with about one hour spent aloft. Experience romance and adventure in the air. (410) 836-1116.

HANG GLIDING
Out on the northern end of Maryland's portion of the Appalachian Trail near Thurmont, there's a sharp crag known as High Top. Jutting from one point overlooking a valley far below is a platform, a kind of runway for enthusiasts of the purest form of wing gliding.

From here, good pilots of the unpowered, kite-like craft can accomplish flights of up to four hours duration, as they utilize slope updrafts and the natural currents known as thermals to gain a mile or so of altitude.

Oregon Ridge Park in Cockeysville is a popular location for beginning instruction in hang gliding. For information call a tape-recorded service at (410) 357-5618.

HELICOPTERING
Montgomery Aviation offers a twenty-minute demonstration hop

183

in a two-seater Robinson R–22 copter, a sight-seeing flight over Washington (or other areas) in the same craft, or flights in a larger Cessna 172. Montgomery County Airpark in Gaithersburg. (301) 258–0090.

"Sky Tours" are offered by Dover International from a base in Reisterstown in a two-passenger Bell 47-G3B2 Wide Cabin Copter. A half-hour flight goes over the Inner Harbor; a longer flight reaches down to Annapolis and back. (410) 561–3500.

LIGHT PLANING

A variety of flight opportunities are available in general aviation light aircraft, many of which are designed as introductions to pilot training.

Hinson Airways offers sight-seeing tours in a four-seat Cessna 172 and demonstration lessons in a two-seat Cessna. BWI Airport. (410) 859–4210.

Another place for light plane rides and training: Brett Aviation at Martin State Airport, (410) 391–0210.

PARACHUTING

Parachutes Are Fun in Salisbury offers a one-day, one-jump training course. (800) 232–9501; or Advanced Aerosports, (800) 526–3497.

Another active parachuting center is Accelerated Free Fall East, located in Chambersburg, PA, not far from Maryland's northern border. (717) 264–1111.

PARASAILING

Hanging from a parachute towed behind a speeding boat is a popular waterside activity. Ocean City has several parasail outfits: Island Para-Sail—(410) 289–2896; O.C. Para Sail—(410) 723–1464; Coastal Para-Sailing—(410) 289–0029. Also available: Bay Parasail, Red Eye's Dock Bar, Mears Point Marina, Grasonville, MD 21638; (410) 827–5299.

SOARING

In recent years, a national group, Soaring Adventures of America, Inc., has advertised gift certificates for introductory flights. Bay Soaring, this region's center, is located in Ellicott City, Maryland (off I-70, west of Baltimore). It offers rides where the glider is released by its tow plane at an altitude of 3,000 feet, 4,000 feet, or 5,280 feet. (410) 781–7050.

Water Sports

SWIMMING

When Captain John Smith explored the Chesapeake Bay in 1608, he noted in his diary "Heaven and earth never agreed better to frame a place for man's habitation . . . truly a delightsome land."

Most swimming within a reasonable distance from Baltimore is in the Chesapeake Bay or its tributaries, for there are no natural lakes within the state.

CHESAPEAKE BAY BEACHES

Bay Ridge Beach, Inc., Herndon Avenue, Annapolis, MD 21403; (410) 267-6363 and (410) 261-2298

Rocky Point Waterfront Park, Back River Neck and Barrison Point Roads, Essex, MD 21221; (410) 887-0217

Fort Smallwood Park, Fort Smallwood Road, Pasadena, MD 21122; (410) 255-5520

Sandy Point State Park, at Chesapeake Bay Bridge, Annapolis, MD; (410) 974-2149

Breezy Point Beach Club & Marina, 5230 Breezy Point Road, Chesapeake Beach, MD 20732; (410) 535-4356 or (301) 855-9894

Betterton Beach, Kent County Parks and Recreation, P.O. Box 67, Worton, MD 21678; (410) 778-1948

ATLANTIC OCEAN BEACHES

Ocean City Visitors & Convention Bureau, Inc., P.O. Box 116, Ocean City, MD 21842; (410) 289-8181 or (800) OC-OCEAN

Town of Ocean City, PR Director, P.O. Box 158, Ocean City, MD 21842; (410) 289-2800

Assateague Island National Seashore, Route 2, Box 294, Berlin, MD 21811; (410) 641-1441

SPRING-FED QUARRY

Oregon Ridge Park and Nature Center, Beaver Dam and Shawan Roads, Cockeysville, MD 21030; (410) 887-1818

CANOEING

Many Maryland State Parks have canoe rentals and canoe trails. For information contact:

Department of Natural Resources, Maryland Forest, Park & Wildlife Service, Tawes State Office Bldg., Annapolis, MD 21401; (410) 260-8186.

C&O Canal National Historical Park, P.O. Box 4, Sharpsburg, MD 21872; (301) 739-4200

River & Trail Outfitters, 604 Valley Road, Knoxville, MD 21758; (301) 695-5177

Patuxent River Park, RR Box 3380, Upper Marlboro, MD 20772; (301) 627-6074

WHITE-WATER RAFTING

White-water rafting on the Potomac and Youghiogheny (in western Maryland) rivers is an exciting and challenging recreation, but should be approached with experience and awareness. It is recommended that you contact a professional outfitter.

Whitewater Adventures, Friendsville, MD; (800) 992-7238

Harpers Ferry River Riders, Inc., P.O. Box 267, Knoxville, MD 21758; (301) 834-8051

River & Trail Outfitters, 604 Valley Road, Knoxville, MD 21758; (301) 695-5177

JET SKI RENTALS

Bob's Sitdown Jet Ski Rental, Wells Cove Road, Kent Narrows, MD; (410) 643-6566

SEA KAYAKING

Water Dogs Kayaking, P.O. Box 918, Sparks, MD 21152; (410) 329-3688

Chesapeake Paddlers Association, P.O. Box 3873, Fairfax, VA 22038

Hiking and Cycling

The State Highway Administration operates a specific bicycle information telephone service, staffed from 8:15 A.M. to 4:15 P.M., Monday through Friday.

HIKING

Appalachian Trail Conference, P.O. Box 807, Harpers Ferry, WV 25425; (304) 535-6331

Backpacking Institute/Hivernan Guide Company, 501 Milford Mill Road, Baltimore, MD 21208; (410) 484-4583

CYCLING

The Best Bike Rides in the Mid-Atlantic, by Judy Bell. The book includes five Maryland bike routes including a covered-bridge ride and a Chesapeake Skipjack challenge. Globe Pequot Press, P.O. Box 833, Old Saybrook, CT 06475.

Bicycling in Maryland. This publication, produced by the Department of Transportation, offers contacts and bicycling information for the entire state of Maryland. (410) 333-1663.

The Maryland Tourism Office produces a cycling map—*Best Bike Routes in Maryland: A County by County Guide.* There are selected routes for each county. (410) 333-1663, ext. 106. In addition, several counties have produced biking tour maps:

The Dorchester County Visitors Guide features a 25-mile Blackwater Wildlife Refuge loop, a 41-mile Vienna to Blackwater loop, and a 6⅓ mile Cambridge loop. (800) 522-TOUR.

Carroll County Classic Country Bicycle Tours includes ten tours with varying degrees of difficulty, through small towns, backroads, and farmlands. (800) 272-1933.

Kent County Bicycle Tours features nine routes ranging from 11 to 81 miles. (410) 778-0416. On Maryland's Eastern Shore, the terrain is especially flat, making bike touring easy, even for novices.

The Beach to Bay Indian Trail is a self-guided tour of Maryland's southern Eastern Shore. It is more than a one-day tour from Baltimore. (800) 521–9189.

C&O Sharpsburg Bicycle Loop maps out a tour that covers the famed Civil War battlefield and segments of the C&O Canal towpath. (800) 228–7829.

The Chesapeake & Ohio Canal Official Map and Guide includes a map of the entire 184-mile biking and hiking trail from Georgetown, near Washington, DC, to Cumberland, in western Maryland. (301) 739–4200.

Bicycle USA Magazine, The League of American Wheelmen, Suite 209, 6707 Whitestone Road, Baltimore, MD 21207; (410) 539–3399

Country Cycling Tours, 140 West 83rd Street, New York, NY 10024; (212) 874–5151

Howard County Bureau of Parks, Centennial Park, 10000 Route 108, Ellicott City, MD 21043; (410) 313–4700

Howard County Bureau of Recreation, Howard County Exec. Center, 3300 North Ridge Road, Suite 170, Ellicott City, MD 21043; (410) 313–2761

Maryland-National Capital Park & Planning Commission, c/o Trails Coordinator/Planning Division, 14741 Governor Oden Bowie Drive, Upper Marlboro, MD 20772; (301) 952–3522

Montgomery County Office of Planning & Project Development, c/o Bike Ways & Trails Coordinator, 10th Floor, 101 Monroe Street, Rockville, MD 20850; (301) 217–2177

Northeast Branch–Indian Creek Park, Maryland-National Capital Park & Planning Commission, Department of Parks and Recreation, 6600 Kenilworth Avenue, Riverdale, MD 20737; (301) 669–4000

Open Road Bicycle Tours, Ltd., 1601 Summit Drive, Haymarket, VA 22069; (703) 754–4152

Washington Area Bicyclist Association, 1015 31st Street NW, Washington, DC 20002; (202) 872–9830

University of MD/Baltimore County, Dept. of Geography, Social Science Building, Room 211, 14741 Governor Oden Bowie Drive, Upper Marlboro, MD 20772; (410) 455-2002

Appalachian Valley Bicycle Touring, 31 East Fort Avenue, Baltimore MD 21230; (410) 837-8068. This company produces complete packages including camping and country inn tours for all levels of ability.

Seasonal Information

Baltimore Area Convention and Visitors Association, Legg Mason Building, 12th floor, 100 Light Street, Baltimore, MD 21202; (410) 837-4636, (800) 837-INFO

Maryland Office of Tourism Development, 217 East Redwood Street, Baltimore, MD 21202; (410) 767-3400

Bureau of Travel Marketing, Commonwealth of Pennsylvania, 453 Forum Building, Harrisburg, PA 17120; (717) 787-5453

The Pennsylvania Historical and Museum Commission, P.O. Box 1026, Harrisburg, PA 17108-1026; (717) 787-2723

Delaware Development Office, 99 Kings Highway, P.O. Box 1401, Dover, DE 19903; (302) 739-4271 or (800) 441-8846

Virginia Division of Tourism, Commonwealth of Virginia, 901 East Byrd Street, Richmond, VA 23219; (804) 786-2051 or (800) 759-0886

West Virginia Division of Tourism and Parks, 1900 Kanawha Boulevard East, Building 6, Room B564, Charleston, WV 25305; (304) 348-2286 or (800) CALL WVA

Regional Information

NORTH

Day Trip 1
Baltimore County Office of Promotion and Tourism, 400 Washington Avenue, Towson, MD 21204; (410) 887-8027

Day Trip 2
Lebanon Valley Tourist and Visitors Bureau, P.O. Box 329, 625 Quentin Road, Lebanon, PA 17042; (717) 272-8555

Day Trip 3
Pennsylvania Dutch Convention and Visitors Bureau (Lancaster County), 501 Greenfield Road, Lancaster, PA 17601; (717) 299-8901 or (800) PA DUTCH

Day Trip 4
Reading & Berks County Visitors Bureau, P.O. Box 6677, Wyomissing, PA 19610; (610) 375-4085 or (800) 443-6610

NORTHEAST

Day Trip 1
Harford County Tourism, 220 South Main Street, Bel Air, MD 21014; (410) 879-2000, ext. 339

Cecil County Office of Economic Development, Room 324, County Office Building, 129 East Main Street, Elkton, MD 21921; (410) 996-5300 or (800) CECIL-95

Day Trip 2

Delaware Development Office, 99 Kings Highway, P.O. Box 1401, Dover, DE 19903; (302) 739–4271 or (800) 441–8846

Greater Wilmington Convention and Visitors Bureau, 1300 Market Street, Suite 504, Wilmington, DE 19801; (302) 652–4088 or (800) 422–1181

Day Trip 3

Philadelphia Convention & Visitors Bureau, 1515 Market Street, Suite 2020, Philadelphia, PA 19102; (215) 636–3300 or (800) 537–7676

Day Trip 4

Chester County Tourist Bureau, Inc., 601 Westtown Road, Suite 170, West Chester, PA 19382–4536; (610) 344–6365 or (800) 228–9933

Brandywine Valley Tourist Information Center, at Longwood Gardens, Route 1, Kennett Square, PA 19348; (610) 388–2900 or (800) 228–9933

Valley Forge Convention & Visitors Bureau, 600 West Germantown Pike, Plymouth Meeting, PA 19462; (610) 834–1550

SOUTHEAST

Day Trip 1

Annapolis & Anne Arundel County Conference & Visitors Bureau, 26 West Street, Annapolis, MD 21401; (410) 280–0445

Day Trips 2 and 3

Dorchester County Tourism, P.O. Box 307, Cambridge, MD 21613; (301) 228–3234

SOUTH

Day Trip 1

Calvert County Department of Economic Development, Calvert County Courthouse, Prince Frederick, MD 20678; (410) 535–4583 or (800) 331–9771

Historic St. Mary's City, P.O. Box 39, St. Mary's City, MD 20686; (301) 862–0990 or (800) SMC–1634

Day Trip 2
Prince George's County Conference and Visitors Bureau, 9475 Lottsford Road, Suite 130, Landover, MD 20785; (301) 925–8300

SOUTHWEST AND WASHINGTON REGION

Day Trip 1
Conference and Visitors Bureau of Montgomery County, Maryland, Inc., 12900 Middlebrook Road, Suite 1400, Germantown, MD 20874–2616; (301) 428–9702 or (800) 925–0880

Howard County Tourism Council, P.O. Box 9, Ellicott City, MD 21041; (410) 313–1900 or (800) 288–TRIP

Day Trips 2 and 3
Prince George's County Conference and Visitors Bureau, 9475 Lottsford Road, Suite 130, Landover, MD 20785; (301) 925–8300

Day Trip 4
Washington, DC, Convention & Visitors Association, 1212 New York Avenue NW, Suite 600, Washington, DC 20005–3992; (202) 789–7000

Day Trip 5
Fairfax County Visitors Center, 7764 Armistead Road, Suite 160, Lorton, VA 22079; (703) 550–2450 or (800) 7–FAIRFAX

Arlington Convention & Visitors Service, 2100 Clarendon Boulevard, Suite 318, Arlington, VA 22201; (703) 358–3988 or (800) 296–7996

Alexandria Convention & Visitors Bureau, 221 King Street, Alexandria, VA 22314; (703) 838–4200 or (800) 388–9119

Manassas/Prince William County, 4349 Ridgewood Center Drive, Prince William, VA 22192–5308; (800) 432–1792

Day Trip 6
Conference and Visitors Bureau of Montgomery County, Maryland, Inc., 12900 Middlebrook Road, Suite 1400, Germantown, MD 20874–2616; (301) 428–9702 or (800) 925–0880

Day Trip 7
Loudoun County Visitor Center, 108 (D) South Street SE, Leesburg, VA 22075; (703) 777-0477

WEST

Day Trip 1
Howard County Tourism Council, P.O. Box 9, Ellicott City, MD 21041; (410) 313-1900 or (800) 288-TRIP
  Tourism Council of Frederick County, Inc., 19 East Church Street, Frederick, MD 21701; (301) 663-8687 or (800) 999-3613

Day Trip 2
Tourism Council of Frederick County, Inc., 19 East Church Street, Frederick, MD 21701; (301) 663-8687 or (800) 999-3613

Day Trip 3
Hagerstown/Washington County Convention & Visitors Bureau, Elizabeth Hager Center, 16 Public Square, Hagerstown, MD 21740; (301) 791-3246 or (800) 228-7829
  Tourism Council of Frederick County, Inc., 19 East Church Street, Frederick, MD 21701; (301) 663-8687 or (800) 999-3613

Day Trip 4
West Virginia Welcome Center, P.O. Box A, Harpers Ferry, WV 25425; (304) 535-2482
  Jefferson County Visitor & Convention Bureau, P.O. Box A, Harpers Ferry, WV 25425; (304) 535-2627 or (800) 848-TOUR
  Tourism Council of Frederick County, Inc., 19 East Church Street, Frederick, MD 21701; (301) 663-8687 or (800) 999-3613

NORTHWEST

Day Trip 1
Carroll County Office of Tourism, 125 North Court Street, Westminster, MD 21157; (410) 857-2983 or (800) 272-1933

Day Trip 2
Tourism Council of Frederick County, Inc., 19 East Church Street, Frederick, MD 21701; (301) 663-8687 or (800) 999-3613

Day Trip 3

Carroll County Office of Tourism, 125 North Court Street, Westminster, MD 21157; (410) 857–2983 or (800) 272–1933

Gettysburg Convention and Visitors Bureau, 35 Carlisle Street, Gettysburg, PA 17325; (717) 334–6274

ABOUT THE AUTHORS

Gwyn Walcoff is president of Chesapeake Communications Group, a marketing and public relations firm in Baltimore. Her worldwide travels have spawned many articles in major newspapers and magazines, as well as radio and television appearances. She authored this book as a tribute to her native land.

Bob Willis is a freelance travel photojournalist who resides in and writes from Scottsdale, Arizona. Formerly Director of Tourism for Baltimore City, he is an active member of the Society of American Travel Writers.